Faith versus Materialism

FAITH
VERSUS
MATERIALISM

The Message of Sūrat al-Kahf

SAYED ABUL HASAN ALI NADWI

Translated by
Mohiuddin Ahmad

Islamic Book Trust
Kuala Lumpur

© Islamic Book Trust 2005

ISBN 978-983-9154-78-8

First published 1973

This revised edition 2005
Islamic Book Trust,
607 Mutiara Majestic
Jalan Othman
46000 Petaling Jaya, Malaysia
ibtkl@streamyx.com
www.ibtbooks.com

First reprint 2007

Cover Design
Habibur Rahman Jalaluddin
bouncegraphics@gmail.com

Printed by
Academe Art & Printing Services

PUBLISHER'S NOTE

The object of this Series is to place within easy reach of students and general reading public, who are not necessarily experts, small handy background books on Islam, taking the reader on an educational journey through its many aspects as a religion and a civilization in all its splendour. These introductory books, we hope, will stimulate interest of the reader to explore further on the subject briefly dealt in these books.

The contents of the books under this Series will be varied—ethical and social, historical and political, philosophical, biographical, and on issues, which are contemporary. We hope these books will contribute to a deeper understanding of Islam and Islam's mission based on knowledge and will help build an integrated approach on the part of Muslims and other readers to serve the cause of Islam and humanity. Insha Allah, God willing.

The author of this little book, Sayed Abul Hasan Ali Nadwi, (1914-1999) was indisputably one of the greatest exponents of Islam in the second half of the twentieth century. Because of his command over Arabic, through his writings and speeches, his influence extended far beyond the Indian sub-continent, particularly in the Arab World. This is an exegesis of *Sūrat al-Kahf* and explains, in the

v

light of the Qur'an, the challenging issues of the modern times and what guidance we can get from this Sūrah to find a solution.

Islamic Book Trust Kuala Lumpur
October 2005

PREFACE

This book was originally written in Arabic and published under the title *Al-Ṣirāʿ bayn al-Īmān wal-Māddiyah* by Dar al-Qalam, Kuwait in 1971 (1390 A.H). It was later rendered into Urdu, like my other Arabic works, by my nephew Muhammad al-Hasani, editor of the Arabic Journal *Al-Baʿath al-Islāmī*, which is published from Lucknow. It has now been translated into English by Mohiuddin Ahmad.

How this book came to be written, what is the nature of exegesis of the *Sūrat al-Kahf* propounded here, from whom have I drawn inspiration in arriving at the conclusions drawn by me, how these are relevant to the challenging issues of the modern times and what guidance can be had from the Sūrah to solve these problems—answers to all theses questions will be found in the following pages. I hope that the book would be found helpful in gaining an insight into the over-all view and the general pattern of the Qur'anic message.

July 2, 1972   Abul Hasan Ali Nadwi
Daira Shah Alam Ullah
Rai Bareli

TRANSLATOR'S NOTE

I write these lines not to flatter myself to introduce this book but to acknowledge my deep gratitude to the author for asking me to render this profound exposition of the *Sūrat al-Kahf* into English. I have read the Urdu version more than once with enlightenment to myself. I thought it desirable that this masterly exegesis of the *Sūrah* which has been widely acclaimed by those who have read it in Arabic and Urdu should be made available in English as well for the benefit of those who want to understand the message of the Qur'an, in general, and *Sūrat al-Kahf*, in particular. The English rendering has also been gone through by the author. Still, if further elucidation is required anywhere for conveying his ideas more accurately, the fault would undoubtedly by mine.

I am also indebted to my friend Mr. Abrar Ahmad Khan who went through the manuscript, like my earlier translations, and helped me in improving and preparing it for the press.

May 3, 1973   Mohiuddin Ahmad

CONTENTS

I. PROLOGUE

My Acquaintance with Sūrat al-Kahf

One of the Sūrahs, or chapters of the Qur'an, that I am accustomed to recite on Fridays since childhood, is Sūrat al-Kahf (The Cave).[1] In the course of my study of the Traditions, I learnt that the Prophet *ṣallā Allāhu 'alayhi wasallam* exhorted his followers to learn and recite this chapter as a means of deliverance from the scourge of al-Dajjāl. This led me to ponder the ways and means, hinted at in this Chapter,[2] which could be the effective method of achieving deliverance from that despicable 'man of sin'; for the Prophet of Islam not only repeatedly beseeched divine protection against him, but also strongly commanded his followers to earnestly seek refuge from that evil. The

---

1. I acquired this habit owing to the insistence of my mother, who always instructed me to recite the Sūrah every Friday, and she ensured from time to time that I was following her instructions. Thus I committed the whole of it to my memory. My mother, who could recite the entire Qur'an from memory, died in Jamādī al-Ūlā, 1388 A. H.

2. It has been related on the authority of Abū Sa'īd al-Khudrī, that whoever recites Sūrat al-Kahf in the way it was revealed, he would be out of the reach of al-Dajjāl. (*Al-Mustadrak lil-Ḥākim*). Another tradition related on the authority of 'Alī, quotes the Prophet of Islam as saying: 'Whoever recites Sūrat al-Kahf on a Friday shall be protected from the evil of al-Dajjāl for eight days, and if the latter appears during this period, he shall be saved from the curse of al-Dajjāl.' Other Traditions promise protection from al-Dajjāl for those who recite the first or the last ten verses of this chapter.

1

Prophet *ṣallā Allāhu 'alayhi wasallam* described al-Dajjāl as 'the greatest evil since the birth of Adam to the Doomsday'.[3]

This naturally aroused my curiosity. I wanted to discover why, of all chapters of al-Qur'an, the Prophet selected this Sūrah for protection against this ominous evil.[4]

The Portending Calamity and Sūrat al-Kahf

I felt an irresistible urge to find the reason for selection of this chapter as a deliverer from the calamity of gathering

---

3. *Ṣaḥīḥ Muslim*, on the authority of 'Imrān ibn Ḥusayn.

4. The Old Testament gives evidence of a general Jewish belief in a hostile person or power who in the end time would bring an attack against God's people—an attack that would be crushed by Jehovah or His Messiah. Psalm 2 gives a picture of the rebellion of world Kingdoms 'against the Lord and against His Anointed'. The same sort of contest is described in Ezekiel 38-39 and in Zechariah 12-14. In the Book of Daniel there are vivid descriptions of the Anti-Christ which find their echo in the writings of the Apostles (cf, e.g. II These 2:4 with Dan 11:36f, and Rev 13:1-8 with Dan 7-8, 20f; 8:24; 11:28,30).

In his eschatological discourse, Christ warns against "false Christs" and "false prophets" who would lead astray, if possible, even the elect (Mat 24:24; Mark 13:22). In Matthew 24:15 he refers to 'the abomination of desolation' spoken of by Daniel.

Paul gives us in II Thess 2:1-12, a full description of the working of Antichrist, calling him 'the man of sin', drawing on the language and imagery of the Old Testament.

In I John 2:18, John shows that the coming of the Antichrist was an event expected by the church. It is apparent, however, that he is more concerned about directing the attention of Christians to anti-Christian forces already at work ('even now are there many antichrists'). He says that teachers of erroneous views of the person of Christ (evidently Gnostic and Ebonite) are antichrists (I John 2:22; 4:3 ; II John 7).

In the Book of Revelation, the Beast of Revelation (17:8) recalls the horned Beast of Daniel (7:8) that claims and is accorded divine homage, and makes war on God's people. With his defeat, the contest of good and evil comes to its final decision.

clouds. I wanted to know what it had to do with the portending evil of al-Dajjāl? Al-Qur'an has a number of chapters of varied lengths, but why was this Sūrah especially selected as a recipe for safety during a period of frightful calamity? [5]

Gradually, I was led to conclude that al-Dajjāl *symbolizes* the abounding evil of the End Time and also that Sūrat al-Kahf provides, more than any other Sūrah, the very means to identify him and guard our spiritual gains against any incursion of this evil. Anyone who desires to comprehend the Sūrah with patience and fullness of knowledge, via frequent recitation and contemplation on the content of its lessons, will undoubtedly be able to guard his soul against that ruthless and insidious wickedness.

This Sūrah clearly reveals the making of the seductive adversary of the End Time, and dwells upon his characteristics so minutely he can easily be identified in every age and place, no matter the form in which he manifests. The Sūrah appraises us of the underlying

---

5. A number of learned doctors of Faith and commentators of the Qur'an, unanimously hold the view that Sūrat al-Kahf is significantly related with the evil of al-Dajjāl. Muhammad Ṭāhir (d. 1578/986) of Paran (in Gujarat), an eminent Traditionalist and lexicographer, relates the view held by earlier doctors that the Hadith extol this chapter as a sheet-anchor of safety against al-Dajjāl, who would appear in the end time. It would afford protection against deceit and cruelty to for all those who would recite and try to understand it, just as the Companions of the Cave were kept safe from the clutches of a ruthless emperor. He adds that the efficacy of the Sūrah is related to its inherent qualities known to the Prophet of Islam (*Majma' Biḥār al-Anwār*, entry: dajl)

thought and content of this evil and its rallying cry, and
further prepares us to withstand and fight this evil—out to
the finish! Thus, Sūrat al-Kahf exposes concepts that
determine this *worldly* attitude of life and society, as put
forth by its own Standard Bearers of these principles of
iniquity, and firmly rejects them as a way of life.

Subject Matter of the Sūrah

When I turned to have a closer look at the Sūrah again,
with the point of view I have just explained, I found that it
presented the actual panorama of a new world, fully
displayed with a range of significance yet unknown to me,
all of which related to but one topic which may be
expressed by the following two phrases: 'The Struggle
between Faith and Materialism' or 'The Invisible Power
and the World of Causation'. The parables and illustrations,
allusions and explanations couched in the Sūrah, all teach
either covertly or overtly, the same lesson on the mystery
of life.

   This discovery filled me with delight! It unveiled a
new aspect of the prophethood of Muhammad and a
recorded miracle of al-Qur'an. I had never imagined that
Scripture revealed in the 6th Cent AD, would vividly depict
features of a Godless Civilization that worked by signs and
wonders to seek Divine worship for itself and ascend to an
over-ripe culmination in the 20th century, though it *came
into the world* in the 17th. This *God-opposing* seductive
agency is personified in the prophetic language as al-Dajjāl,

a tyrant: resisting and denying the over-lordship of God while tending to deify its own political power, and was graphically described centuries before it saw the light of day!

I put forth my views in an article written about 35 years back[6] when I was teaching exegesis of the Qur'an at the Nadwat al-'Ulamā', Lucknow. The article was published by Sayyid Abul A'la Mawdudi in his journal *Tarjumān al-Qur'ān*. I also had an opportunity to stay at Hyderabad for a short while in 1946, as a guest of the late Sayyid Manāzir Ahsan Gīlānī, the then head of the Department of Theology in the Osmania University of Hyderabad. This provided me an opportunity to discuss the matter with M. Gīlānī who had read my article. He intended, as he then told me, to write a detailed commentary of this chapter of the Qur'an for publication in the monthly journal *al-Furqān* of Lucknow. The said journal did publish his entire article, albeit and alas, posthumously.

I then felt inclined to expand my thesis after going through the lengthy article of M. Gīlānī which had been published years after my earlier paper. I intended to highlight the inspiring theme of the Sūrah which is closely connected with the underlying concept of philosophical thoughts and intellectual movements of the last age. From that perspective, I hoped to focus attention on the signs, lessons and notes of warning contained in the Chapter;

---

6. This was written in 1973.

undoubtedly taking advantage of the masterly exposition of
the Sūrah by M. Gīlānī. However, I have not followed the
conventional pattern of the Qur'anic commentaries. On the
contrary, this is an exposition of my own thoughts and
impressions of the Sūrah's content.

Key to the Personality of al-Dajjāl

The name of Antichrist, known as al-Dajjāl[7] in Arabic,
provides a clue for the comprehension of those hidden
traits, characteristics, and features, of a *concept* whose
distinguishing marks signify evil, mischief, apostasy, and
enmity towards God. Therefore, falsehood and deception
are the two central notions from which radiate the
attributes, characteristics, functions, and mission of what is
symbolized in the person of al-Dajjāl.

The distinctive trait that embodies today's
materialistic civilization is fraud and a swaggering denial
that belies its dominance in every walk of life. Not a
single aspect of life today is free from its contaminating

---

7. Ibn Manẓūr writes in *Lisān al-'Arab*, the largest Arabic lexicon, that *al-
dājil* from which Dajjāl is derived means a liar or a deceiver. Al-Dajjāl is also
called the *False Christ* because the spell of his falsehood will be the most
potent means of his deception. Abū 'Amr whose explanation of the word is
regarded as the best by Ibn Khālawayh, says that al-Dajjāl, being a cheat or a
swindler, resembles a plate coating of a base metal with silver or gold to
deceive others. Al-Azharī too agrees with Abū 'Amr and holds that al-Dajjāl
signifies an outward appearance or show that hides reality. For this reason,
gold coating is also termed Dajjāl. Abū al-'Abbās says that al-Dajjāl is so
named because he would deceive others by preserving falsehood in the most
attractive manner.

influence. Things are presented exactly by opposite names. A jumble of high-sounding names, nomenclatures, clichés, and terminologies, all abound to the extent of meaninglessness! What's more is that the outward appearance has hardly any relation to whatever content lay within: whether it be the beginning and the end, the objective in view, the means adopted to realize it, or ideals and concepts reverently put forth; *and* the conduct of their propagators are all diametrically opposed to what is propagated.

Similar is the case of all those philosophies, or more accurately, jargons, which have bewitched people and taken the place of religion. An aura of inviolable sacredness is established around teachers and the *pronouncements* of these mentors. Love and respect for them and their doctrines of faith are actually demanded as *articles* of faith, and the expression of the least doubt in their greatness or eminence is dubbed reactionary or an obscurantist denial of well-known and accepted facts! And this is not only true of the populace and laity, but even the most intelligent and highly educated elite, can be seen singing the praise of modernist ideologies without giving thought to the sincerity or truthfulness of its proponents, or any dispassionate evaluation of the harm or good these ideologies have done to humanity.

Lacking in both moral courage and intellectual integrity, they are carried away by the fallacious claims of these ideologies, and in pursuit of these illusive ideals, they

remain completely oblivious to any end results obtained
from the endeavour: whether it be for well-being or its
absence! All this is the product of the hypnotizing of a
deceitful delusion conjured by seductive agencies that are
mere forerunners of the Great Deluder, who is terribly more
powerful and irresistible in whatever time or clime he
might make his appearance.

This spirit of falsehood, deceit, and artful trickery
pervades modern civilization simply because it has turned
its back on the over-lordship of God, the office of
prophethood, the unseen realities, and divine revelation.
Decidedly, today's society chooses to depend exclusively
on the senses and perceptible realities, and has reposed its
trust in the earthly pleasures, immediate gains, power, and
pelf! And this is what the Sūrah seeks to contradict. The
events recounted therein, along with the parables alluded in
this chapter, point to the same moral: the brevity,
uncertainty, and vanity of the worldly life, with its traps
and delusions.

Role of Judaism and Christianity

We have to acknowledge the fact, albeit regretfully, that
despite fundamental differences in their faiths and beliefs,
the roles of Christianity (which lighted the path of Europe
during the medieval ages) and the revengeful Judaism have
been more or less complementary in the making of present-
day materialistic civilization. Both are, to be sure, equally
responsible for pushing humanity towards an extremist and

uncompromisingly materialist outlook of life, which
essential ingredients are denial of ethical-spiritual values
and doctrine of the Prophets.

The Christian nations of the West which had thrown
off the yoke of Papacy by the end of the 16th Century and
severed relations with the true Christianity that preached
Unity of God and clemency, adopted a purely utilitarian
concept of life. The rapid strides in technological
discoveries and the manufacture of devastating weapons,
coupled with a complete imbalance between knowledge,
emotion, intellect, conscience, business, and morals have
now confronted humanity with the imminent danger of its
swift annihilation.

The world Jewry took a keen interest in the recent past,
owing to a variety of causes pertaining to their racial pride,
educational advancement, political ambitions, etc., to
accelerate the pace of technological progress. This has
enabled them to assume control of modern civilization.
They have gained the start in every field: literature,
education, political thought, practical politics, press and
industry—in fine, they have become the torch-bearers of
modern Western culture and its way of life; even a cursory
survey of recent developments in international politics
convince us of the pivotal role played by world Jewry in
Western society.

With all its treasure of knowledge and glittering
progress, this civilization is now rushing ahead towards its
doom: a product of unyielding despair and negative views

on life. This is to happen then because of the Jews, who have been allowed, regardless of their defiant and vengeful predisposition along with treacherous 'cloak-and-dagger' methodologies, to strengthen their roots in the nutritious soil of Western society. The modern West has afforded them opportunity to nurse and flourish in the *secret springs* of Jewish life, in a manner they never had in the past. This is the tragedy of modern times: a grave and menacing challenge—not only to Arabs who are presently faced with the life and death struggle owing to it, but also to the entirety of mankind, as we must all confront the approaching danger!

This is perhaps the reason why this chapter of the Qur'an is intimately connected with the beliefs of the Jews and Christians. The Sūrah begins with a reference to what the latter regards as the most important article of their faith:

"Praise be unto Allah Who hath revealed the Scripture unto His slave, and hath not placed therein any crookedness, (but hath made it) straight, to give warning of stern punishment from Him, and to bring unto the believers who do good works the news that theirs will be a fair reward, wherein they will abide for ever; and to warn those who say, Allah has chosen a son, (a thing) whereof they have no knowledge, nor (had) their fathers. Dreadful is the word that cometh out of their mouths. They speak naught but a lie." (Q, 18:1-5)

Christianity is the cradle of a modern civilization that is passionately fond of the earthly life and its comforts, and which pays undue emphasis to the material welfare. This covetous civilization has rejected all ethical-spiritual values and has impetuously plunged headlong to capture power and glory, gold and riches. And this is the ground where Judaism finds its meeting-point with Christianity, despite its differences and enmity with the latter.

One hardly finds any clear-cut references to the Hereafter, Day of Judgement and requital, preparation for the eternal abode of bliss, description of Paradise and its rewards, finite nature of earthly life, denigration of covetousness, contempt for power and pelf, condemnation of fomenting trouble and strife, or exhortation to adopt such moral virtues as contentment, righteousness and piety in the verbose narrations of the Old Testament! Absence of any emphasis in the Old Testament on the fleeting nature of earthly sojourn in this terrestrial world and the eternal rewards and/or punishment in the Hereafter makes it conspicuously different from other revealed scriptures.

It is therefore not at all surprising, that the history of Jewish people finds expression in the *will for power* for power's sake—in addition to thirst for revenge, pangs of jealousy, racial pride, covetousness, egotism, and chauvinism! All these inclinations and propensities are fostered and stimulated by their religious scriptures, literature and history. We also find visible traces of these in their thoughts, philosophies, political movements, discoveries, and intellectual endeavours. Likewise, their general code of social conduct has no place for such values and sentiments as humanitarianism, generosity, self-abnegation, benevolence, forbearance, detachment from worldly pleasures, or longing for reward in the Hereafter.

For these very reasons, God has sternly admonished the Christians for their adoptionist belief in regard to Jesus Christ that makes him an associate in the Divinity of God. They have also been warned against the scramble for worldly goods and fleeting pleasures.

"Lo! We have placed all that is on the earth as an ornament thereof that We may try them; which of them is best in conduct." (Q, 18:7)

Administering a reproof to those who deny the Hereafter and place confidence in their worldly possessions, the Qur'an says:

"Say: Shall we inform you who will be the greatest losers by their works? Those whose effort goeth astray in the life of the world, and yet they reckon that they do good work." (Q, 18:103-4)

Unflinching belief in the Hereafter, unseen realities, and the Creator of the Universe and His Omnipotence is thus the central theme of Sūrat al-Kahf. In its rationale, motive and Judgement, this belief runs counter to the spirit, ideation and conception of the materialist view of life, a view that places confidence only in the senses and their perceptions. The latter vociferously extols earthly benefits, sensual pleasures, and racial/national superiority, while the Sūrah scornfully rejects these as abominably loathsome! In this wise, the Sūrah drives home the uncertainties and paradoxes of our earthly life, for it is this *worldly attitude* of the Christian nations that has led them, more than any other people, to promote and patronize the materialist world-view.

After the Christians, the Jews have assumed its direction and patronage, although they have been the greatest adversaries of Christianity since its inception. Now this civilization is destined to attain its culmination under inspiration and guidance of the Jews, one of whom will undoubtedly show signs of the Great Antichrist or *al-Dajjāl al-Akbar*, by overshadowing all other standard-bearers of deceit and falsehood, irreligion and godlessness.

The Prophet of Islam is reported to have said that the recitation of this Sūrah, particularly its initial portion, would save one from the evils of al-Dajjāl. There is a sequence and significance in the initial and closing verses of the Sūrah that are easily discerned. The Sūrah, as a whole, is thus intimately connected with the scourge of al-Dajjāl. The contents of this Sūrah can be divided into four parts which unfold its central theme:

(1) The story of the Companions of the Cave.
(2) The parable of the owner of two gardens.
(3) The story of Prophet Moses and al-Khiḍr.
(4) The story of Dhū al-Qarnayn.

The Two World-Views

There is a natural and necessary relationship between cause and effect (consequence) in all physical phenomena. In other words, the cause contains the sum total of circumstances which inherently result as its effect: i.e., this sum total pre-exists as a *potential* that gives rise to the consequence or effect. *Cause* and *Effect* are thus inter-dependent contingencies, and the former, almost always in given circumstances, lead to the manifestation of the latter. Now—there are people, who never look beyond the basic causal dependence, and who limit themselves to the analysis of speculative thought or scientific observation. Their view, therefore, is restricted by the material: i.e., the *perceptible* objects and events.

Naturally then, these people believe in a universal causative origin of all phenomenon. To them, no effect or consequence can appear without the cause, nor do they recognise any power which may intervene between cause and effect. They maintain the universality of all cause-effect relationships as existing 'outside' or 'independent' of any Intelligent Being that might introduce or modify the effect, with or without the cause, in accordance with its will. This view implies a denial of everything else save matter, which to them, is the common source of the origin of all that exists or takes place. Thus do they either deny or discount the existence of the Creator: the Lord of the Universe Whose writ runs supreme in the cosmos!

Consequently, this denial extends also to His Omnipotence, The Day of Judgement, and Life after Death.

Therefore do they devote their energies to discovering the *necessary relationship* between the cause and its effect, or the *common source* of diverse natural phenomena, and of matter and its properties and physical laws, with a view to *commanding* these forces of nature. Unfortunately, their overweening quest to capture the matter makes them slaves of the material world. Matter then, becomes the Alpha and Omega for them! Everything else, including consciousness, mind and intellect become thereby a product of matter: a reflection of the *external* material world.

When they gain control over some of these forces, they put them in requisition for selfish ends and behave as demigods, claiming lordship over the life and property of others, either in their own right or on the name of a society, party, or nation. Nothing can then deter them from inflicting the most horrible tortures on their fellow human beings, especially those whom they brand with infamy for opposing their cherished social or political views of life.

But there is another worldview, and it is essentially different from the one described above in its basic postulates; a view that offers solutions to fundamental questions of philosophy. It proceeds from the principle that apart from the causes and effects that manifest as physical laws of matter governing substance and its properties, there is a transcendental omnipotent power that predetermines all cause and effect. Functional dependence of the cause upon this All-Pervasive Power is as absolute and exclusive as that of the effect on the cause. Every physical phenomenon, event, and incident depends wholly on the Will and Pleasure of God, Who brings into existence whatever He likes from non-existence, with or without primordial cause. He creates conditions for the action of the cause, and if He so desires, severs the functional relationship between the objects themselves, because: the relationship exists in the world of phenomena by the Will of God, and therefore also exists outside-of and independent-of matter! He is thus the Supreme Cause—the Cause of all causes.

The creation of planetary systems and causative law does not make the universe free, even for a moment, from the absolute control of its Creator—nor is it capable of becoming so. The so-called causative origins of phenomena have never been a whit more than passive instruments designed to perform the Will of God! Nor were they ever endowed with an objective character capable of freeing themselves from the bonds of Divine bondage. No material object can claim freedom of action nor cast off its shackles, for it is God, Who has, with His infinite wisdom, united not only properties with material objects, but also causes with their inevitable consequences. Verily, He alone creates and annihilates, unites and separates, and brings into being whatever He likes out of naught.

"But His command, when He intendeth a thing, is only that He saith unto it: Be! and it is." (Q, 36:82)

This holds out a consistent view of nature and society—of social life as well as natural phenomena. At the same time it recognises imperceptible yet far more potent effectual causes that shape human conduct and determine the destiny of nations. The operation of *these* causes is remarkably more effective, and their effects more extensive and momentous than those attending visible causal relations and environments. These operative agencies are faith, righteous action, ethical conduct, justice, equity, mercy and love, and unflinching submission to God; all working together against *other* intangible dark forces as represented by atheism, godlessness, cruelty, selfishness, vice, sinfulness, sedition, and sabotage.

Anybody betaking himself to these spiritual-moral norms without disregarding the physical laws of nature, shall find the entire cosmos cooperating with him and assisting the achievement of his objectives. Divine succour shall bear a hand to him, and not un-seldom, even the physical laws of causation shall be made subservient to his purpose. Celestial miracles shall unfold themselves to espouse his cause, while on the contrary, whoever shall rely solely on physical laws without regard to the spiritual-ethical norms of morality, shall ultimately find the entire universe standing against him. The very forces of nature he has captured shall defy and deceive him. Instead of being subservient; these shall be hard on him, and his dependence upon artificial contrivances will go on increasing till he is debased by the most pitiful servitude of his own making.

Sūrat al-Kahf:

A Story of Struggle between Faith and Materialism

Sūrat al-Kahf is the story of an unending struggle between these two ideologies or concepts which are diametrically opposed to each other. One is the materialism that denotes the primacy of objective existence in the external substantial world; the other asserts the existence of realities which lie beyond the range of human perception, by virtue of the existence of God and the interaction of moral-spiritual forces, etc... The Sūrah explains the meaning and purpose of faith with relation to Ultimate Reality, and warns men against leaning exclusively on observable environments, grounds and consequences, that eventually lead to the denial of God and His Authority.

II. THE STORY OF THE CAVE

Of the four stories told in this Sūrah, the first one relates to the Companions of the Cave. Who were these Companions?—what is the moral and wisdom concealed in the story?—why did the Qur'an verify the tale—and why has man yielded to its fascination ever since it was recounted? These are some of the questions which ought to be given thought for gaining an understanding of the Sūrah.

The Christian Sources

Before we narrate the story as told by the Qur'an in its own inimitable manner, presenting only the core of the tale intertwined with moral lessons, admonitions, warnings and good tidings—let us look at the olden traditions and hagiographical literature handed down in regard to this legend. Thereafter, these versions can be compared with the Qur'anic description, in order to find out how much they corroborate or contradict the story as told by the Qur'an.

The story of the Cave does not find a place in the Old Testament since the events are reported to have occurred in the earlier phase of the Christian History. This was the time when the faith of the Christians was matured and their number was fast multiplying, owing to the fiery zeal of the earliest followers of Jesus Christ. By that time, even the later books of the Old Testament had been compiled, and therefore, the Jews could hardly be expected to preserve the legend in their scriptures. On the other hand, this fascinating story was divinely inspiring for Christians, who were irresistibly carried away by its charming mystery and electrifying character.

The story furnished an ennobling example of the living faith of *primitive* Christians, and reveals an unfaltering adherence to revealed truth and readiness to sacrifice everything for the sanctity of their religious precepts. It held a meaning and lesson for those believers who considered it their birthright to assert the inalienable right of conscience. Furthermore, the story remains an exhortation and inspiration, and awakens even today the spirit of sacrifice and struggle for the defence of one's faith and way of life. These distinctive features of the tale make it an immortal drama, capable of stirring large numbers of people in different times and climes.

This also explains why it was handed down so meticulously by one generation to another. Now, we have to see the details of the story, as extant in a number of languages and differing versions which pertain to the early Christian sources, in order to discover what early narrators of the story thought of it. Below is an outline of the story as summarised by Ignaza Guidi for the Encyclopaedia of Religion and Ethics, taken from the earliest Christian sources:

"The legend of the Seven Sleepers is one of the most wide-spread and pleasing of hagio-graphical legends. The elements of the story common to the earliest text are briefly as follows:"[1]

"The Emperor Decius comes to Ephesus[2] and there revives the worship of idols, commanding that all, and especially the Christians, should offer sacrifices to them; some Christians abjure the faith, others remain steadfast and suffer tortures. Seven youths (or, according to some texts eight[3]) who live in the imperial palace, and whose names are variously given,[4] are accused of being secretly Christians, and, when brought before Decius, refuse to sacrifice to the idols. In the hope that they might waver in their resolution, Decius grants then a respite and then leaves Ephesus. The youths

---

1. Edward Gibbon's description of the story in *The Decline and Fall of the Roman Empire*, vol. III, pp. 413-14 (London: 1908) discusses the sources and historicity of the event but unnecessarily also gives vent to his prejudice against Islam and its Prophet.

2. An ancient Ionian city on the west coast of Asia Minor situated near the modern village of Ayasoluk (Seljuk) in the Izmir *il* of Turkey. In historic times it was located on the lower slopes of the hills, Croesus and Peon, which rise out of the fertile plain near the mouth of river Cayster. The temple of Artemis or Diana, to which Ephesus owed much of its fame, was in the plain about one mile north-east of Peon (modern Panjir Dagh). The Romans had made it the capital of their West-Asiatic possessions and it rose to become a well-known trade centre of its day. The cult of Artemis combined, like other idolatrous forms of worship elsewhere, with the stinking pleasures of the flesh. (For further details see Blackie's *A Manual of Bible History*.)

3. Cf. M. Huber, Die Wanderlegende Von den Siebenschlufern, (1910) p. 9 ff.

4. Huber, pp. 91, 492.

leave the city and hide in a cave in the
neighbouring Mount Achilus. One of them,
Diomedes (or Iamblichus), disguised in rags goes
down to the city to enquire about what was
happening in it and to buy food. Decius, returning
after a short time to Ephesus, orders the youths to
be conducted to his presence. Diomedes informs
his companions of the order; sadly they take food,
and then they all fall by divine Providence into a
deep, long sleep. When Decius cannot find the
youths in Ephesus, he summons the parents, who
try to excuse themselves for the flight of their sons,
and tell that they are hidden in a cave in Mt.
Anchilus. Decius orders the entrance of the cave to
be blocked with large stones, so that the youths
may be buried alive. Two Christians, Theodore
and Rufinus, write the story of the young martyrs
on metal plates, which they place under the stones
closing the cave. After 307 years[5], during the reign
of Emperor Theodosious II, a heresy breaks out,
led by Bishop Theodore, denying the resurrection
of the dead, and the emperor is greatly perturbed.
Then God suggests to Adolius, the proprietor of
the field where the cave is, to build a sheepfold for
his flocks; for this purpose the workmen use the
stones which close the entrance of the cave and

---

5. For variants (353 years, etc.) see Huber, p. 100f.

thus the cave is reopened. God awakens the youths, who think they have slept only one night, and who exhort each other in turn to suffer martyrdom at the hands of Decius, if need be. Diomedes goes down to Ephesus as usual, and is so surprised to see the cross over the gates of the city that he asks a passer-by if it is really Epesus. He is anxious to return to his companions with the news, but first he buys food, paying for it with the money he had about him, which was of the time of Decius. The vendor and the market people, seeing the ancient money, think that the youth has found a hidden treasure and wish to share it with him: they drag him with threats through the city; many people assemble, and the youth looks in vain among them for some of his acquaintances. The bishop and the governor question Diomedes, who narrates the whole story and invites them to come to the cave and see his companions. They climb the hill and find the two tablets of lead which confirm the youth's story; then they enter the cave and find the companions alive and shining in appearance. Theodosius is informed of what has happened and comes to Ephesus to the cave. One of the youths, Maximilian, (Achillides or others) tells him that, in order to demonstrate the truth of resurrection, God had caused them to fall asleep and then resuscitated them before the Judgement

Day: after this the youth fall asleep in death.[6] A
basilica was erected on the spot."[7]

In so far as the historicity of the legend is concerned,
neither critic has been able to prove it as entirely baseless,
nor has anybody demonstrated it as a 'flight of
imagination'. The story is extant in a number of versions:
Greek, Syriac, Latin, Coptic, Arabic, Armenian, Ethiopic,
and Georgian—and there is also no reason to doubt the
authenticity of the ancient texts. Edward Gibbon, who
normally gives little credence to the miraculous and
outlandish stories, writes of this legend as follows:

"The origin of this marvellous fable cannot be
ascribed to the pious fraud and credulity of the
modern Greeks, since the authentic tradition may
be traced within half a century of the supposed
miracle. James of Sarug,[8] a Syrian bishop, who
was born only two years after the death of younger
Theodosius, has devoted one of his two hundred

---

6. The story has also been told by Ibn Jarīr al-Ṭabarī and other commentators
of the Qur'an on the authority of Muhammad ibn Ishāq, but owing to the
absence of adequate details and also the more reliable sources discovered
later, a good many myths had been introduced by them vide *al-Tafsīr
al-Kabīr*, vol. XV, pp. 123-6. The original Christian sources have therefore
been given preference.
7. *Encyclopaedia of Religion and Ethics*, (1934) art. "Seven Sleepers", vol.
XI, p. 428.
8. James, one of the orthodox fathers of the Syrian Church, was born A.D.
452; he began to compose his sermons, A.D. 474; he was made bishop of
Batnae, in the district of Sarug and province of Mesopotamia, A. D. 519, and
died A.D. 521 (Assemanni, tom. i, pp. 288, 289). For the homily *de Pueris
Ephesinis*, see pp. 335-9.

and thirty homilies to the praise of the young men of Ephesus. Their legend, before the end of the sixth century, was translated from the Syriac into the Latin language by the care of Gregory of Tours. The hostile communions of the East preserve their memory with equal reverence; and their names are honourably inscribed in the Roman, the Abyssinian, and the Russian calendar. Nor has their reputation been confined to the Christian world."[9]

The duration of the time spent by the Companions of the Cave in deep slumber has been variously given in different versions. Some Christian writers reckon it to be 353 or 373 years, but the general consensus is that the youths slept for a period ranging from 300 to 307 years. In round numbers, 300 years in the solar calendar would come to 309 in the lunar calendar. Ibn Kathīr is of the view that the number of years spent in the cave, from the time the youths miraculously fell into sleep to the time they were awakened, was made known to the Prophet of Islam through revelation. The period given by Ibn Kathīr too is 300 years according to the solar calendar, and 309 according to the lunar calendar. He further says that since every hundred solar years are equal to one hundred and three of the lunar calendar, the Qur'an says: "and added nine" after "three hundred years".

---

9. Edward Gibbon: *The Decline and Fall of the Roman Empire*, vol. III, pp. 413-14.

Most of the Christian sources—as well as Gibbon and
Muslim writers—hold the view that it was during the
persecution by Decius (A. D. 250), who is known as
Daqianus to Arab historians the youths concealed
themselves in the cave. Decius is known to have instituted
an organised persecution of the Christians throughout the
Roman Empire. The second sovereign mentioned in the
traditions is Theodosius II (408-450 A. D.) in whose reign
the youths are reported to have been awakened. Taking 250
A. D. and 450 A.D. we get an interval of 200 years,
whereas the traditions give this period as one hundred and
eighty-seven years. Gibbon, relying on these, exercises his
wit to ridicule the period mentioned in the Qur'an. Some of
the earliest as well as recent commentators of the Qur'an,
for instance, Jamāluddīn al-Qāsimī and Abul A'la
Mawdudi, have tried to explain away this apparent
contradiction by putting forth the view that the words
"three hundred and add nine", mentioned in the Qur'an,
simply repeat the then current traditional view instead of
indicating a definite period of the deep slumber of the
youths. They argue that the above-mentioned passage is to
be read in the context of the preceding verses: "(Some) will
say: They were three, their dog the fourth,"

This view is attributed to Qatādah and Muṭrif ibn
'Abdullah. The commentators who prefer this interpretation
also point out the succeeding verse which says: "Allah is
best aware how long they tarried." Their contention is that
if God had revealed the exact period, He would not have

drawn attention towards His Own perfect knowledge immediately after the verse in question. This exegesis is ascribed to Ibn 'Abbās. But al-Alūsī, another commentator, points out that since Ibn 'Abbās accepts the number of the Companions of the Cave as seven, he ought to have considered number of years too, for, both the verses mentioning the number of the companions and the period of slumber are followed by a similar warning that the true knowledge is with God alone.[10]

There are, however, several other eminent commentators of the Qur'an who do not agree with this explanation. They hold the view that it is not correct or acceptable to put a construction on any verse which is not explicitly clear, excepting those explained in elaborate details. Imām al-Rāzī, the commentator of the Qur'an, says in his *Tafsīr al-Kabīr*:

"The verses intervening between the revelation: 'Some will say: They were three, their dog the fourth ...' and the verse giving out the number of years, *show that the two are entirely unconnected.* On the other hand, the verses: 'So contend not concerning them except with an outward contending,' and 'Say: Allah is Best Aware how long they tarried', do not refer to tradition or fable mentioned earlier. These can, therefore, only mean that instead of relying on what others (Jews and

---

10. *Rūḥ al-Ma'ānī* (*Sūrat al-Kahf*).

Christians) say, one should pin one's faith in the
revealed truth."

Shaykh al-Islām ibn Taymiyyah has this to say:

"The words:[11] "Say, Allah is Best Aware", indicate
that the view taken by certain commentators that
the Qur'an was quoting the traditions (in regard to
the period of sleep) current among the Jews and
Christians is erroneous. The period indicated is not
a repetition of what others say—it is a revelation
from God."[12]

It has to be remembered that the so-called discrepancy
pointed out by Gibbon regarding the period of sleep
mentioned in the Qur'an, proceeds from the assumption
that the youths concealed themselves in the cavern during
the Decian persecution. Decius was proclaimed emperor in
September 249 A.D. and died in June, 251 A. D. It seems,
most probably, that Decius was *assigned* the role of villain
in this tragic drama by later scribes. This is most likely due
to his atrocious cruelty in the persecution of Christians who
disobeyed his edict to perform a pagan religious sacrifice[13]
in the presence of duly appointed commissioners, who were

---

11. *Al-Tafsīr al-Kabīr*, vol. III.

12. *Al-Jawāb al-Ṣaḥīḥ liman baddala Dīn al-Masīḥ.*

13. See *Encyclopaedia Britannica* (1968), vol.I, p.157, art. "Decius". It was,
however, not under the reign of Decius but much earlier, under Trajan (98-117
A. D.), that those accused of Christianity were directed to offer sacrifice to
heathen gods. Those who refused to do so were to be punished for a crime and
exposed to capital punishment. Under Trajan were martyred Symeon, Bishop
of Jerusalem, and Ignatius, Bishop of Antioch. (George H, Dyer: *History of
the Christian Church*, New York-1896, vol. I, pp. 65-66)

then to issue a certificate (*libellus*) that they had done so. This imperial edict is reported to have been issued in June, 250. Early in 251, a few months before the death of Decius, the Commissioners seem to have ceased their activities.

Decius, who ruled for less than two years, had to spend the greater part of his brief rule amidst the cares of war: first against the Emperor Philip and then against the Goths. The final engagement took place on a swampy ground in the Dobruja in June 251 and ended in the defeat and death of Decius.[14] He perhaps never had the time to visit his far off eastern dominions; at least the accounts of his rule given by historians are silent about any such excursion.

Ecclesiastical writers of the fourth or fifth centuries, seem to have exaggerated the earlier martyrdoms owing to an unrelenting zeal that filled their breasts against idolaters of their own times. Gibbon says, on the authority of Origen, the number of early martyrs was very few, and that under the rigorous persecution of Decius only ten men and seven women suffered for their profession of the Christian faith.[15] These accounts are, however, silent about any persecution of the Christians in or around Ephesus on the orders of Decius.

It seems the hiding of these Christian youths was a *local* affair, of too minor a significance to attract the

---

14. *Historians History of the World*, (London,1908), vol. VI, pp. 413-14 and Edward Gibbon: *The Decline and Fall of the Roman Empire*, (London-1909), vol. 1, pp. 246-50.

15. Gibbon: *The Decline and Fall of the Roman Empire*, (London-1909), vol. 11, p. 98.

attention of the historians. To the contrary, their miraculous
awakening after the prolonged sleep, accompanied by their
dramatic appearance in the city and presentation before the
authorities, must have been a memorable affair raising a
tumultuous commotion in the entire Christendom! The
story of the Seven Sleepers, with its reminiscences of
classical mythology, must have captured the imagination of
clergy and laity, as well as poets and historians, making it
one of the most enchanting fables of the day. The point of
the story does not, therefore, lie in the name of any given
Emperor mentioned by later scribes but in the fact that the
beginning of the period of slumber coincided with the reign
of an Emperor who persecuted the Christians.

Viewed from this angle, it seems highly probable that
the Seven Sleepers hid themselves in the reign of Hadrian[16]

---

16. Hadrian learnt on August 11, 117, while in Syria, of Trajan's death, then
assumed the government. For 12 of his 20 years as emperor, Hadrian was
absent from Rome, which was perhaps the most notable feature of this
principate. In 121 Hadrian left Rome on his first travels. He first toured the
west and then the east. Traversing Asia Minor, he returned by way of Sicily to
Rome by the end of 126. The next year was spent at Rome, and after a visit to
Africa, he set out on his second great journey in September 128, travelling by
way of Athens. In the spring of 129 he again visited Asia Minor and Syria,
where he invited the kings and princes of the East to a meeting at Samosata.
Having passed the winter at Antioch, he set out for the south in 130. He
ordered Jerusalem to be rebuilt under the name of Aelia Capitolina, to be
peopled with gentile Roman citizens, and then made his way through Arabia
to Egypt. Hadrian returned through Syria to Europe, but was obliged to hurry
back to Palestine to deal with the Jewish revolt that broke out in 132. For a
while he commanded the field himself, then in 134, leaving the conduct of
affairs in the hands of Julius Severus he returned to Rome. He died at Baiae on
June 10, 138.

(P. Aelius Hadrianus) who donned the imperial purple for a fairly long time from 117 to 138. In April of 129, Hadrian undertook a long journey to the eastern provinces of the empire from which he did not return to take up his residence on the Tiber until the year 134. It is not necessary that the persecution of the Christians of Ephesus should have taken place in the presence of Hadrian or even under his orders. In the extensive dominions of the Roman Empire, any magistrate who exercised in the provinces the authority of the emperor, or of the senate, and to whose hands alone the jurisdiction of life and death of the subjects was entrusted, could have behaved as a remorseless tyrant. It is not improbable that some such functionaries of the State, stimulated by motives of avarice or personal resentment, might have been more zealous in enforcing the royal edict. This is no mere assumption, for we can find analogous examples in every age.

Palestine blazed with its last and the most desperate rebellion for three years during the reign of Hadrian. When the end came in 135, Palestine was a ruined and largely depopulated country. The holy city was henceforth prohibited to the Jews.

Hadrian was proud and vainglorious, envious and destructive, hasty and vengeful, inquisitive into other men's affairs, and often induced by sycophants to acts of cruelty and injustice. He permitted the revival of the persecution against the Christians, and showed many instances of a bad disposition, which it was the whole study of his life to correct or to conceal. (*The Historians' History of the World*, (London-1908), vol. VI, p. 281.)—"Hadrian was no old Roman", writes George H. Dyer, "but a modern spirit: curious, religious and sceptical—he maintained Trajan's policy, but cautioned against wholesale accusations." (*History of the Christian Church*, New York,1896, vol. 1, p 66

We can thus reasonably conclude that the Companions of the Cave concealed themselves during the reign of Hadrian and were raised from their deep slumber in the time of the younger Theodosius. This, if agreed, would not only bring the Christian traditions in conformity with the period indicated in the Qur'an, but also sap the very foundations which provided Gibbon with an opportunity to deride the Divine revelation. And this appears to be all the more reasonable because no extant source is definite about either *beginning* or *end* of the prolonged sleep of the youths. There is also wide variation between the periods reckoned on the basis of various sources by different authorities. The Syriac sources, for example, claim that the Seven Sleepers woke up in 425 or 437 A. D., while Greek traditions fix the incident in 446 A.D., or the 38th year of the reign of Theodosius II. It is our unalterable faith that the Qur'an, being the true custodian of earlier scriptures, is much more trustworthy than all those ancient texts which were always open to changes and corruption.

The persecution of the Christians, who were falsely charged with burning the Roman capital and subsequently punished with the most horrid tortures, was initiated by Nero as early as 64 A.D., and this continued unabated under Trajan, Hadrian and Marcus Aurelius. There were occasional periods of peace during the long years of persecution, which lasted till Constantine embraced Christianity in the beginning of the fourth century. The perplexity produced by the scant and discordant historical material about the early years of Christianity is another reason not to place reliance, as did Gibbon, on any particular tradition or ancient accounts in regard to the exact period and dates of the prolonged sleep of the Seven Sleepers. After all, the hiding of a small band of unknown persons in a far off province of the Empire would have been a minor incident of no significance. Their awakening, on the other hand, during the reign of an Emperor who professed the Faith of the persecuted fugitives, must have stirred the imagination of the people!

The real significance of the story can be realised however, in the context of the then raging controversy about the resurrection of the body and retribution in the Hereafter. Irrefutable evidence by virtue of an awesome demonstration of 'Life after Death' was indeed required to revive belief in Resurrection. This event *did happen* to proclaim this Eternal Truth, and soon became the most popular and widely circulated story throughout the Roman Empire. As could be hoped in such circumstances, the story circulated from mouth to mouth, and would necessarily have become somewhat vague in regard to details and the dates, *before* it was reduced to writing.

Why the Story was re-told in the Qur'an

The reason for the revelation of Sūrat al-Kahf, as related by Muhammad ibn Ishāq, is reported to be certain questions asked from the Prophet Muhammad peace and blessings be on him by the idolaters of Mecca—who were instructed by

the Jewish rabbis to do so—as a test of his prophethood.[17]
One of the three questions thus asked by the Meccans
related to the Companions of the Cave. Even if this
Tradition were correct, it cannot be regarded as the sole
reason for the selection of an event, amongst innumerable

---

17. Ibn Jarīr relates on the authority of Ibn 'Abbās that the Quraysh had
deputed Naḍr ibn al-Hārith and 'Uqbah ibn abī Mu'īṭ to the Jewish doctors of
Yathrib to ask them about Muhammad and his teachings, since the Jews were
considered custodians of ancient scriptures and also possessed the knowledge
of the prophets of yore. The story has also been related by Marmaduke
Pickthall, who says that when the two delegates arrived in Yathrib, they told
the Jewish rabbis about the character and teachings of Muhammad and begged
them to inform if he was to be believed. The Jewish doctors instructed them to
ask three questions; for they said, Muhammad would answer them correctly
only if he were a true prophet.
"Ask him," said the Rabbis, "of some youths who were old, what was their
fate, for they have a strange story; and ask him of the much-travelled man
who reached the limits of the east and west, what was his history; and ask him
of the Spirit, what it is. If he is able to answer these questions correctly, then
follow him; if he is unable to give correct replies then treat him as an
impostor."
The two emissaries then turned back to Mecca and told the Quraysh that they
had returned with a crucial test for Muhammad. They put all the questions to
Muhammad, as directed by the Jews. The Prophet said that he would surely
answer them upon the morrow, without adding 'if it pleases God'. As reproof
for that omission, the wished-for-revelation was withheld from him for fifteen
days. The Quraysh bitterly reproached the Prophet for his failure to answer the
questions, but at length Gabrial brought the revelation (Sūrat al-Kahf)
containing replies of all the three questions. The revelation contained an
admonition for the Prophet's grief, as well as the stories of the youths and the
much-travelled man. It also repeated the question put by the idolaters about
the Spirit: "They will ask thee concerning the Spirit, Say: The Spirit is by
command of my Lord, and of knowledge ye have been vouchsafed but little"
(Qur'an 17:85). It is, however, to be noted that one of the intervening narrators
of this Tradition 'Ikrimah, from whom Ibn Isḥāq relates it, not being
trustworthy, it cannot be treated as perfectly authentic.

incidents of unbridled cruelties in the name of religion, for narration in the Qur'an. The events normally regarded as the *immediate cause* of a revelation of *any* particular Sūrah, and sometimes given undue emphasis by certain doctors of religion, are not given much weight by eminent commentators.

The Qur'an was, in truth and reality, revealed for exposition of the Truth and presentation of the Divine Guidance which man had lost because of his negligence and wickedness. The natural inclinations, propensities, and dispositions of man have not undergone any notable change; he still needs, as ever, the same intellectual and moral bases of the Right Path which were revealed to earlier prophets and which reached their eventual consummation in the teachings and the life of the last Prophet, Muhammad, on whom be peace and blessings of God. This is the cogent reason and underlying cause, being much more potent and intelligible than any isolated incident narrated as a background for any particular piece of revelation. Shāh Walīullah (d. 1176/1763), one of the greatest savants of the Qur'an, has gone at length to explain this fact:

"Normally, the commentators of the Qur'an describe some incident or event to explain the background of the verses dealing with or containing divine commands, as if it were the sole reason for the revelation of that particular verse. It is, however, an accepted fact that the central theme and the chief object, for which the Qur'an has been revealed, are the guidance of mankind, the eradication of heretical beliefs, and the abandonment of immoral practices. The existence of these vices among any people is, thus, a sufficient reason for the revelation of divine guidance and commandments. Cruelty and wickedness of any people provide, in the same way, the ground for revelations designed to eradicate these evils. Reckless disregard of the bounties of God or obstinate indifference to the portents mentioned in the Qur'an are, in fact, the chief reasons for revelation of verses conveying grim warnings to the evil-doers. Except for those incidents which have been hinted at in any particular verse, and which happened during the life-time of the Prophet or earlier, there is really no need to go into those details which have been laboriously gone into by certain commentators of the Qur'an."

Sūrat al-Kahf was revealed at Mecca at a time when the small band of helpless Muslims was facing almost the same type of religious persecution which had led the Companions of the Cave to hide themselves in a cavern from the fury of the then Roman Emperor. A picturesque description of the conditions then obtaining in Mecca, preserved in the Qur'an, illustrates the perilous situation of

the Meccan Muslims—and this can perhaps apply equally
to the youths of Ephesus seeking refuge in the cave:

"And remember, when ye were few and reckoned
feeble in the land, and were in fear lest men should
extirpate you..." (Q, 8:26)

The collections of the Prophet's Traditions and his
biographies are replete with incidents of untold oppression
and atrocious persecutions inflicted on his followers—
Bilāl, 'Ammār, Khabbāb, Muṣ'ab, Sumayyah and others.
These atrocities are fiendish enough to pain and bruise
every sensitive heart. The mounting wave of barbarous
oppression was met by exemplary endurance of the faithful;
yet, without a ray of hope and being tired of the ceaseless
tortures, the patience of the poor victims was reaching its
breaking point. Caught in the frightful claws of devouring
brutality, the Meccan Muslims were placed, literally
speaking, between the devil and the deep sea. Their
struggle for life and death has been deftly depicted by the
Qur'an:

"... When the earth, vast as it is, was straitened for
them, and their own souls were straitened for them
till they bethought them that there is no refuge
from Allah save toward Him." (Q, 9:118)

It was precisely at this moment of despair that the
divine revelation descended with a comforting and soothing
message, rehearsing a tale of miraculous succour to the
oppressed, holding the promises of prosperity after
adversity, comfort after suffering, and victory after defeat.

The meaning and lesson of this wonderful story lay beyond the accepted categories of human experience and speculation, and enters the ultimate reality—the positions of tyrant and victim—and demonstrates how God delivers a small oppressed band of helpless youths from the tyranny of an encircling violence of passionate, capricious, formidable, and easily inflamed fury: a violence possessing all the sinews of power and position, wealth and glory. It disclosed how God brings out the dead from the living, and life from the dead, turns a furious and blood-thirsty enemy into a gracious and affectionate ally, and allows a believer to profit by the inheritance of a non-believer.

Meccans Muslims and the Companions of the Cave

In this darkest hour of despair and helpless melancholy, the Qur'an narrated to the Meccan Muslims the stories of Joseph and his brothers, Moses and Pharaoh, and the Companions of the Cave. The first was the tale of a Prophet raised from slavery to kingship; the second was the story of a nation and its Prophet clasped in the clutches of a tyrant king; and the last one spoke of a handful of helpless youths subjected to the most gruelling test by a cruel oppressor. These tales differ from one another in so far as time, circumstances, and the principal actors of these sinister dramas are concerned, but the common chord of similar objectives and identical ending runs through them all. Each tale demonstrates how the overruling will of God imposes itself in some inscrutable and incomprehensible way, and how He allows the believer to gain ground upon the non-believer, the God-fearing upon the blasphemer, the victim upon the tyrant, and the poor upon the rich. Divine justice is very often dispensed in such wise, as to leave no doubt of God's omnipotence! Here is the moral drawn from the story of Joseph by the Qur'an:

"In their history verily there is a lesson for men of understanding. It is not tale invented but a confirmation of the existing (Scripture) and a detailed exposition of everything, and a guidance and a mercy to such as believe." (Q, 12:111)

After recapitulating the story of Prophet Hūd, the Qur'an says:

"And all that We relate unto thee of the story of the messengers is in order that thereby We may make firm thy heart. And herein hath come unto thee the Truth and an exhortation and a reminder for believers." (Q, 11:120)

When we consider the appallingly desperate situation in which the Muslims of Mecca had then been placed, a striking similarity appears between them and the Companions of the Cave. These youths of Ephesus concealed themselves in the cave to preserve their faith and worship, remaining there till the inevitable end of the most powerful Empire of the day; an Empire governed by numerous zealous tyrants and guided by the most amiable and philosophic characters—an aristocracy that disdained all consideration of justice or moral virtue, and submitted the innocent and passively obedient followers of Jesus Christ to horrible tortures. But at last, the Seven Sleepers awoke during the reign of an emperor whose respectable attachment to the Gospel urged him to further the interests of true religion and restore justice to those whom it had been denied earlier.

The Muslims of Mecca also endured the most bitter trials and tribulations under the scorching sun; as if standing on the lava of violence until divine succour came in the form of permission to migrate from Mecca. They were allowed to take shelter in the spacious 'cavern' known as Yathrib. However, God had destined His new fugitives to accomplish a greater and more glorious task than that given to His earlier servants: these Meccan exiles were chosen to disseminate and flourish the message of God to the four corners of the world.

> "He it is Who hath sent His messenger with the guidance and the religion of truth, that He may make it conqueror of all religion however much idolaters may be averse." (Q, 61: 9)

The *Apostleship* of Muhammad therefore, did not merely signify consummation of prophethood in his person; it also charged his followers with the responsibility imposed on the earlier prophets.

> "Ye are the best community that hath been raised up for mankind. Ye enjoin right conduct and forbid indecency; and ye believe in Allah." (Q, 3:110)

The Prophet too, on whom be the peace and blessings, directed the Muslims thus:

"You have been sent to relieve and not to create difficulties."[18]

Although a minority, the town of Yathrib was not only too small a place for the believers, it was also cut off from the mainstream of life in Arabia. The fact was that the future of humanity depended on these persons who were—using a phrase coined by Jesus Christ, (peace be upon him)—'the salt of the earth'. This small band of believers was destined to resuscitate a dying world and breathe fresh life into it. God had, therefore, decided to preserve these persons, though He did not make them to fall into deep slumber like the Companions of the Cave, or allow them to renounce the world and live like hermits. On the contrary, they were burdened with the responsibility of preaching the religion of God, of fighting falsehood and irreligion, and of asserting the supremacy of the One and Only God over everything else.

"And fight them until persecution is no more, and religion is all for Allah." (Q, 8:39)

When Diomedes, one of the Companions of the Cave, came out of his cavern, he found an entirely new world; it was so different that he could no longer recognise the once familiar landmarks of his native city! The lad was astonished to find the Christian Cross over the gates of Ephesus and the country ruled by an Emperor of his own

---

18. *Al-Tirmidhī* on the authority of Abū Hurayrah.

Faith. Likewise, when the Meccan refugees went back to their native city, they found the banner of Islam fluttering over the city, the keys of Ka'bah in the hands of the Prophet, the humiliated religion being held in the highest esteem, and the idols worshipped by the pagans demolished and destroyed. Those who had been forced to leave Mecca as humiliated and harassed emigrants were now received on their return with honour as the benefactors of humanity. Viewed in this light, we find striking similarities between the Companions of the Cave and the refugees of Mecca. Whatever the apparent dissimilarities, they are due to differences of location and era of the two incidents, the variant character of the two peoples, and the distinctive teachings of the two faiths.

History Repeats Itself

God has ordained Islam to flourish in eternity and its votaries to survive, transmit, and diffuse His message to the end of time. It is therefore beseeming that it should pass through a confrontation with all circumstances faced by earlier nations. Its call necessitates the combat of those obsessions, prejudices, and hatreds that always obstruct the way of righteousness. It is therefore no wonder that on varying occasions we find Islam victorious, defeated, powerful, weak, acclaimed, and reproached. Like the poor and persecuted followers of almost every prophet, we persistently see movements trying to have Islam disbanded and dispersed; sometimes through administrations avowedly anti-Islamic, and on other occasions, by governments claiming the stature of Islamic States.

The rulers of so-called Muslim or Islamic states take pride in Islam, construct palatial mosques, solemnly commemorate the birthday of the Prophet, and celebrate the *'Īds*; but along with these they also entertain a mortal fear for the true and unalloyed faith and its actual practice. Strange though it may seem, these rulers consider Islam and the way of life it enjoins even more dangerous for their existence than atheistic philosophy or heathen practices. Wherever such unscrupulous rulers come into power, the drama of the Seven Sleepers is re-enacted in the very lands of Islam, and once again an arduous struggle ensues between the weak, small, and helpless minority of devout believers and a powerful majority of hypocrites. The story of the Companions of the Cave then again yields a striking and needful lesson for the Muslim youths.

"Lo! they were young men who believed in their Lord, and We increased them in guidance. And we made firm their hearts when they stood forth and said: Our Lord is the Lord of the heavens and the earth. We cry unto no god beside Him, for then should we utter an enormity." (Q, 18:13-14)

Sometimes horrifying circumstances make it difficult for a believer to choose between his life and the freedom of his conscience. A true Muslim is then left with no alternative but to withdraw from society and lead a secluded life. Such a perilous situation may arise only occasionally, perhaps once in centuries, but the prophethood of Muhammad, being the perfect and eternal guidance vouchsafed to mankind, not only identifies such dismal circumstances but also provides adequate direction to face them. The Prophet of Islam made this prediction:

"A time will soon come when the best possession of a Muslim will be his goats with which he will seek asylum in a valley or in the hills for the sake of his faith."[19]

These are the occasions when Sūrat al-Kahf comes to the rescue of the believer and illuminates the path he ought to tread.

We will now present the story of the Companions of the Cave as recounted in the Qur'an. Although the Qur'an gives only an outline of the story and excludes unnecessary or irrelevant details, in its own inimitable style it displays in the liveliest colours the main theme of the story, in order to illustrate significant implications and underlying morals.

Idol Worship and Licentiousness

In the days of early Christianity, Ephesus was a city of gods celebrated for the occult arts and gross sensuality. History bears an irrefutable witness to the intimate affiliation of idolatrous cults and licentiousness—as though the former depends for its existence on the latter! If we look at the archaeological remains of the ancient cities of India,

---

19. *Al-Bukhārī*, on the authority of Abū Saʿīd al-Khudrī.

Greece, Egypt, or pagan Arabia, we readily appreciate this connection clearly. And so it also happened in Ephesus, where the pagan tradition of Artemis debased all moral sentiment. A grossly materialistic society thus came into existence in the centre of the Eastern Empire that justified ideals of sensual enjoyment, satisfaction of desire, immediate gain, and the primacy of an external, material world. This ideology, with the help of political and economic powers at its command, conquered the hearts of the populace since it offered riches, respect, and authority to its votaries. Manners and morals of the ruling class, as ever, fascinated the common people and gave rise to a sophisticated caste that was clearly bent upon gratifying carnal desire in servitude to the achievement of power and pelf while climbing ladders of authority, no matter the cost!

The government of the day explicitly supported the pagan traditions and ceremonies as the common culture of the land.[20] It was indignant against anyone who referred to them as idolatrous and impious, or opposed the prevalent forms of worship and moral ideals. It vindictively punished those who separated themselves from the mainstream culture

---

20. Speaking of the Roman society in the days of early Christianity, says Gibbon: "The religion of the nations was not merely a speculative doctrine professed in the schools or preached in the temples. The innumerable deities and rites of polytheism were closely interwoven with every circumstances of business or pleasure, of public or private life; and it seemed impossible to escape the observance of them, without, at the same time, renouncing the commerce of mankind and, all the offices and amusements of society." (*Decline and the Fall of the Roman Empire*, vol. II, p. 16).

and traditions, by removing their rights of citizenship or imposing capital punishments on them. The opulent society of the Roman times abounded with superstitious observances and pursuits of pleasure, and allowed no freedom of conscience, in order to impress upon all citizens a common stamp. It wanted to level down all people into a homogeneous lot, an undifferentiated, identical reproduction of the same culture, manner, and morals.

Courageous Believers

In the midst of this environment of oppressive luxury, dominated by a powerful government polluted by the stains of idolatry, there were also men of upright nature who responded to the call of Jesus Christ as soon as it reached them. The precepts of the gospel so powerfully captured the heart and soul of the early Christians that it became impossible for them to live without their Faith. They could not barter away their beliefs for any price—not even at the cost of their lives—and therefore they withstood every persuasion and persecution to wean them from their Faith.

These were the reasons that first gave rise to a deep disquiet, an inner struggle in the hearts of Christians which manifested itself in a valiant tussle with the forces of evil. They had, of necessity, to chalk out a way of their own as dictated by their faith and moral precepts, directly opposed though it was, to the demands of the Empire.[21] The

---

21. "Every Christian rejected with contempt," says Gibbon, "the superstitions of his family, his city, and his province. The whole body of Christians

government was fervently idolatrous, and was averse to tolerate anything other than heathen cults. The society coveted every pleasure which might gratify the sensual; neither would it be satisfied with an enjoyment less voluptuous and surfeited. And, obviously, if anybody, led by seemingly petty scruples of religious belief, dared to provoke the displeasure of the ruling class and society, it became difficult for him to earn his bread.

Every apparent consideration—the demands of social life, the grim facts of worldly existence, etc.—compelled one to adopt the manners and morals of the pagan society. The unerring logic of observable phenomena endorses the prevailing psychology of the masses: i.e., that one ought to 'ride high on the hog's back'. Their arguments, as ever, are that man cannot live without bread, and bread cannot be had without money; therefore, one should seek favours of the powers that be. Respect, power, and glory go with the offices of state, so why not try to achieve *these*, if you can? Peace and security are the essential prerequisites of one's existence, for that reason one should purchase them—even if it demands conforming to the popular traditions and beliefs of the community.

---

unanimously refused to hold any communion with the gods of Rome, of the empire, and of mankind. It was in vain that the oppressed believer asserted the inalienable rights of conscience and private Judgement. Though this situation might excite pity, his arguments could never reach the understanding, either of the philosophic or the believing part of the Pagan world. To their apprehensions it was no less a matter of surprise that any individual should entertain scruples against complying with the established mode of worship, than if they had conceived a sudden abhorrence to the manners, the dress, or the language of their native country." (*Decline and the Fall* ... vol. 11, p. 75.)

But, if someone rejects with unyielding temper the persistent logic of things, those facts accepted as incontrovertible and inescapable by others, it can only be because his gaze is transfixed by certain transcendental truths beyond the reach of the senses but nevertheless divulged via the power of his pristine faith. He knows that in addition to any causative apparatus possessed by governments and society, there is yet another more potent generative cause in the hands of the Creator of causes; the very Will of God—the originating propelling force behind all ostensible relationships between cause and effect, ground and consequence.

Where the Will and Pleasure of God avails to furnish its support, the law of phenomenal causation becomes ineffective. The Creator of the world, the Omnipotent Lord, can cause the world, time and space to change their natural course for His bondsmen whom He desires to help, in order to create favourable situations and circumstances as He likes, and to bestow abundant blessings on whomever He wills. One need not, therefore, bend in submission to anyone other than God, nor espouse the causes that are themselves weak and ineffective. All one needs is a firm, unshaken faith in the Omnipotent Lord. Indeed, it is this conviction that moves mountains and subdues materialistic urges, through a sincere belief that annihilates the logic of reason via the logic of faith. And this is the essence or pith of the story of the Companions of the Cave.

"Lo! they were young men who believed in their
Lord, and We increased them in guidance. And We

made firm their hearts when they stood forth and said: Our Lord is the Lord of the heavens and the earth. We cry unto no god beside Him, for then should we utter an enormity. These, our people, have chosen (other) gods beside Him though they bring no clear warrant (vouchsafed) to them. And who doth greater wrong than he who inventeth a lie concerning Allah?" (Q, 18:13-15)

The Life without Faith

But the question is how were they enabled to cling to their faith in the face of an insurmountable opposition— disowned by their native land, rejected by their government and society, and denied all means of subsistence? They had no choice before them. The ghastly alternative open to them was either a life without faith or a faith without the vital flame of life and freedom of conscience. In a situation as frightening as this, faith came to their rescue and fortified the conviction that the earth is wide enough to provide refuge to them. They should, therefore, cut themselves adrift from all the benefits and pleasures, and pin their faith in the help of God alone.

"And when ye withdraw from them and that which they worship except Allah, then seek refuge in the Cave; your Lord will spread for you of His mercy and will prepare for you a pillow in your plight." (Q, 18:16)

The Correct Way of Migration

It was surely possible that the Muslims of Mecca could have stealthily dispersed to seek shelter in a cavern or upon the summit of a hill. They could also have very well lived like hermits, as did degenerate Christians of the medieval ages who had decided to re-direct the course of their spiritual life. However, God helped them to take the correct decision, that is, to *leave* their native land, *collectively*. Seeking succour from God, it was thus that they departed from the city to preserve their faith, their religion, and their mode of worship while pinning their faith in God, being *confident* of His relief in their distress. This was the same admirable course adopted by the Companions of the Cave, and manifestly demonstrates the way to be adopted by all believers, when placed in similar dreadful circumstances threatening their faith and religion.

The Reward of Lasting Conviction

And what is the outcome of such a steadfast conviction? When the two preconditions of unshaken faith and courageous defiance of evil are fulfilled by a believer, Divine succour descends from the clouds to render relief in his sufferings. "They were young men who *believed* in their Lord," says the Qur'an. The reward of their unflinching belief is further described in the words of God: "We increased them in guidance."

This was not a solitary incident, for it happens every so often. When a Muslim revolts against the grinding tyranny of an intolerant society and government, above all he needs courage, patience and divine guidance, and his most pressing need at that moment is the solace of peace for his bruised heart. This explains why and how God made the Companions of the Cave able to stand resolutely firm before the persecuting tyrant. Their agitated heart was made secure; their fear, hesitation, and despair were replaced by courage, determination and confidence. Indeed, these supreme armaments are ever required by upholders of faith, who have always to struggle against irreligion and godlessness.

And then the question arises: What reward did the youths of Ephesus get for bidding farewell to their city, its delightful pleasures, their means of living, and the distinguished families[22] they hailed from?

The first proof of their affectionate regard by God came in the form of a spacious and healthy cave[23] to which Providence guided them for shelter. To excavate such a spacious cavern in the hills in those days would have been most difficult, requiring a tremendously disciplined and costly effort. The cave itself was a most suitable and

---

22. Al-Alūsī writes in the *Rūḥ al-Ma'ānī* that the youths belonged to affluent and respectable families. (vol. V. p. II).
23. The Arabic word used is *kahf*, which denotes a *spacious* cave or hollow place in a rock. A less spacious and small cave is known as *maghārah* (*Lisān al-'Arab*).

natural dwelling, being bright and airy, without excessive heat or cold.

> "And thou might have seen the sun when it rose
> above away from their Cave to the right, and when
> it set go past them on the left, and they were in the
> cleft thereof."[24] (Q, 18:17)

The Companions of the Cave had thus been allowed to sink into sleep in a cool and comfortable environment—the best they could desire of benefit from our terrestrial world at that time. And furthermore, their retreat to safe shelter and induced sleep, had for all practical purposes joined them in communion with a world other than their own; a world untouched by mere phenomenal cause and effect, undisturbed by despicable despots and tyrants. This was a crowning reward for their unflinching faith and splendid courage. The Qur'an alludes to this blessing from God in these words:

> "That was (one) of the portents of Allah. He whom
> Allah guideth, he indeed is led aright." (Q, 18: 17)

Atheists and those who disbelieve in the sovereignty of God, direct their energies, knowledge and efforts to harness the forces of nature, in order to make their life more pleasant and comfortable. However, the results accruing are more often disappointing. They find themselves afflicted

---

24. Al-Alūsī says that the youths slept well inside the cave, unperturbed by the sun and its heat. (*Rūḥ al-Maʿānī*, vol. V, p. 20) Imām al-Rāzī says that the cave opening to north would have the sun on its right when it rose and on its left side when it set.

with anxiety and bewilderment, confusion and misery, despite the triumphs of splendid discoveries and the abundant conveniences of their material prosperity. Defeated and disappointed by their own achievements, they seem to be sinking into the morass of anxiety and psychological diseases, illness and lunacy, and a trembling before the bewildering spectacle of dreadful weapons that threaten their own existence. The Qur'an symbolises this truth in these words:

> "And he whom He sendeth astray, for him thou wilt not find a guiding friend." (Q, 18:17)

Their Spiritual Existence in the Cave

Neither did they lack divine guidance in the cave, nor were they doomed to an *inert* spiritual existence. It seems that they had with them certain inscriptions, perhaps pages of the Old and New Testaments) containing prophetic guidance.[25] This again is a sign to all who are forced to

---

25. The Qur'an speaks of the cave as well as of al-Raqīm, or the Inscription. What is meant by this word the commentators differ; some consider it to be the stone slab placed near the mouth of the cave, on which the names of the youths were inscribed, others are of the opinion that it was the name of that town or city. Manāzir Ahsan Gīlānī has expressed the view that these were the pages of scripture taken by them into the cave with them. A tradition related on the authority of Ibn 'Abbās has been quoted in *Rūḥ al-Ma'ānī* (vol. V, p. 11) which says that it was a book containing the religious teachings of Christianity. We are inclined to this view for it is supported by another Tradition, handed down by Ibn Jarīr on the authority of Ibn Zayd that "the *Raqīm*" means a book, but the secret of this book has not been revealed by God. (vol. V. p. 122). Imām al-Bukhārī, too, agrees that the *Raqīm* was a book.

migrate from hearth and home for the sake of their faith.
When the youths had spent the provisions they had brought,
they were lulled to deep sleep by God.

> "Then We sealed up their hearing in the Cave for a
> number of years." (Q, 18:11)

Transformation of the Roman Empire

The establishment of Christianity as the public religion in
the entire length and breadth of the Roman Empire, was an
event signifying the greatest miracle among the wonders
connected with the story of the Seven Sleepers. During the
prolonged period of their miraculously deep slumber, the
Christian gospel was embraced and diffused in the far-flung
provinces of the Empire. The stains of idolatry and sensual
enjoyment are totally denounced, and people began to look
askance upon those who once claimed high marks of
distinction for devoted zeal to idolatrous cults. A new way
of life, that of faith in Jesus Christ,[26] raised its head from
the gloom of heathen cults and frivolous dissipation that
had settled upon Roman society. Christianity, long
regarded as a despised faith visited with the most frightful
punishments, now generally inspired people to esteem and
reward the merits of its followers. The Seven Sleepers were

---

26. The emperor Constantine I, the Great, who ascended the throne in 306, is
believed to have embraced Christianity for what appears to have been a
mixture of personal and political motives. He convened councils of bishops to
bring about uniformity in the creeds and beliefs of the Christians and founded
the city of Constantinople in 324, dying in 335.

thus permitted to awake after more than three hundred years of deep and comfortable sleep.

> "And (it is said) they tarried in their Cave three hundred years and add nine." (Q, 18:25)

They asked each other: "How long have we slept?" But since none of them was able to indicate the exact duration of their sleep, they gave up the barren controversy as it was important neither for their religion nor for their worldly life.

> "A speaker from among them said: How long have ye tarried? They said: we have tarried a day or some part of a day. (Others) said: Your Lord best knoweth what ye have tarried." (Q, 18:19)

After a while, pressed by the call of hunger, they decide that one of them should secretly return to the city to bring food for them. They hand over the coins they have with them to purchase the best food.[27]

> "Now send one of you with this your silver coin unto the city, and let him see what food is purest there and bring you a supply thereof." (Q, 18:19)

They think the situation has not changed and that they are still fugitives, hotly pursued by the state officials. Therefore, they ask their companion to be extra cautious and to be courteous.

---

27. The best food, as explained by al-Imām al-Rāzī, means a pure and wholesome food. This also denotes that the wholesome food is permitted by the Sharī'ah and is not an impediment in attaining spiritual merit.

"...Let him be courteous and let no man know of
you. For they, if they should come to know of you,
will stone you, or turn you back to their religion;
then ye will never prosper." (Q, 18:19-20)

The people of Ephesus had still not forgotten the
youths, who had, in their opinion, sacrificed their life for
religious faith. They knew how they had been sealed up in
the cavern, never to come out again. The nascent Christian
empire under Theodosius II, on the other hand, was
inflamed by the fervent spirit of devotion to its new faith. It
wanted to consecrate and glorify the sacrifices of its earlier
saints and martyrs. There could, then, be no other incident
worthy of a higher regard and noble remembrance than that
of the Companions of the Cave.

Fugitives Turn into Heroes

The youth sent to buy provisions secretly arrives in the city
like a runaway slave. He wants to return to the cave as
early as possible, but suddenly he finds himself and his
companions in the spotlight of fame and honour. The
old-fashioned dress, obsolete language and the ancient
money which the youth has with him, at once draw the
attention of the people to him. The Qur'an does not go into
all these details, as its purpose is not to rehearse the story
but to draw out its moral. The news, however, spreads like
wild fire and the people, the bishop, the governor and the
Emperor himself, hasten to visit the cavern to have a
glimpse of the sacred place. The Qur'an, as usual, does not

give the details of the profound esteem commanded by the Seven Sleepers, but expounds the lesson:

"And in like manner We disclosed them (to the people of the city) that they might know that the promise of Allah is true, and that, as for the Hour, there is no doubt concerning it." (Q, 18:21)

The solemn revolution in the government and populace of the Roman Empire, and the discovery of the forsaken youths of Ephesus after such a long time, signified the way God fulfils His promise and ultimately confounds the anti-God forces. The event furnished a proof that God is the Lord of the world, of time and space and can change the situation whenever He likes.

"And because the Hour will come, there is no doubt thereof; and because Allah will raise those who are in the graves." (Q, 22:7)

Who could have imagined that the forces of tyranny would wither away providing the most favourable circumstances for the expansion of the harassed and persecuted Christianity? Nobody could have similarly visualised that the Companions of the Cave would one day be re-discovered, youthful and beaming with a holy radiance, to confirm Christian faith in the Resurrection of the dead. Which of them knew, that when they were a hunted and persecuted lot, they would again be received by their countrymen with the worshipful respect paid to the sovereigns? Was there, also therefore, no moral in the story for the over-confident chiefs of Mecca, or no sign of hope for the weak and persecuted followers of the Prophet?

The youths of Ephesus remained alive till they had
delivered the message for which they had been roused from
their deep slumber. The message delivered, they again fell
asleep. Their followers could not agree on the type of
memorial to be established to preserve their memory.

"When (the people of the city) disputed of their case
among themselves, they said: Build over them a
building; their Lord knoweth best concerning them.
Those who won their point said: We verily shall
build a place of worship over them."[28] (Q, 18:21)

A basilica erected on the spot was not the only
memorial of these youths. The memory of the youths was
preserved with reverence and made the object of several
homilies and *acta martyrums*, and their names were
honourably inscribed in the Roman, the Abyssinian, and the
Russian Calendars.[29]

"(Some) will say: they were three, their dog the
fourth, and (some) say: Five, their dog the sixth,

---

28. "Certain persons justify construction of shrines," says al-Alūsī in his
commentary of the verse, "but it is prohibited and a sacrilegious act." Al-
Bukhārī, Muslim and Al-Nasā'ī have related a Tradition from 'Ā'ishah, and
there is another one recorded by Muslim on the authority of Abū Hurayrah,
which says: "May God censure the Christians and the Jews who turned the
graves of their prophets into places of worship." Imām Ahmad, al-Bukhārī,
Muslim and al-Nasā'ī add that such persons would be the worst afflicted lot
on the Day of Judgement. The verse only tells us what had then happened and
does not at all justify their emulation, particularly, since we do not know if the
persons referred to were pious or not. It is possible that the decision might
have been taken by the king or one of his grandees (*Rūh al-Ma'ānī*, vol. V,
pp.31-32).
29. Edward Gibbon: *Decline and the Fall* ... , vol. III (London, 1908), p, 414.

guessing at random; and (some) say: Seven, and their dog the eighth. Say (O Muhammad): My Lord is Best Aware of their number. None knoweth them save a few. So contend not concerning them except with an outward contending, and ask not any of them to pronounce concerning them." (Q, 18:22)

Victory of Faith over Materialism

Out of the four stories recounted in the chapter 'Al-Kahf,' this first marvellous tale comes to an end here. It clearly describes the struggle between faith and materialism; in other words, it identifies differing consequences for placing confidence in causes rather than in the Creator of causes. It demonstrates how faith overcomes materialism and awakens a deep and sincere conviction in the Ultimate Cause of all causes.

Those believing youths of Ephesus preferred faith over the materialistic view of life, and opted for the promised reward of the Hereafter rather than the immediate gains in earthly life. They chose poverty and faith rather than power and pelf that were dependent upon profane idolatry. They did not allow the pagan cult to tarnish their spirits and debase their sentiments even though they had to bid farewell to their native land or to friends and parents, and they denied themselves the popular admiration of their privileged position, as well as the allurements of pleasure. Instead of yielding passively to the forces of tyranny and sinful infidelity, or to licentiousness of desire and fickleness of reason, they elected to bend in submission before the worthy demands of their innermost self.

Their choice was final and without reservation, and the subsequent events proved that the decision taken by them was sagacious, well-considered, and correct. They also demonstrated the truth that eventual success is assured to those who fear God; who prefer Him over the apparent trappings of phenomenal causation and are willing to face every hardship to uphold their ennobling faith. The lesson was brought home by the imperishable faith of the Companions of the Cave, who endured the persecutions with indomitable courage and matchless fortitude until the empire persecuting them embraced the gospel of Jesus Christ.

This is a story which is repeated time and again by the unending conflict between faith and a 'way of life' characterised as "the world" and its terminal stages. The story of the Companions of the Cave, therefore, seeks to demonstrate that causes and effects are subservient to the will of God, and that they have been fashioned to ultimately uphold faith and righteous action. The correct way for the believer, therefore, is to pin his faith in the omnipotence of God and seek His blessings through unflinching conviction and righteous action.

Before going over to the parable of the Owner of Two Gardens, the Qur'an bids the Prophet to hold fast the rope of divine guidance and cling to unalterable faith in Him.

This is the way of God as shown by the Qur'an and illuminated by earnest faith. It commands the Prophet to seek the companionship of those believers who manifest unfailing faith and who delight in the recollection of God, even if they share an insignificant portion of worldly riches and material possessions. It asks him to refrain from the company of such ignorant and insensible persons, who, although endowed with position and rank, are denied the blessings of faith and prostration of the soul.

The Qur'an addresses the entire humanity through the Prophet of Islam. Its message is for every believer who would ever need these solemn teachings for adopting the path of righteousness:

> "Restrain thyself along with those who cry unto their Lord at morn and evening, seeking His Countenance; and let not thine eyes overlook them, desiring the pomp of the life of the world; and obey not him whose heart We have made heedless of Our remembrance, who followeth his own lust and whose case hath been abandoned." (Q, 18:28)

Like the Companions of the Cave, true believers in every age have given preference to their faith, and to righteous behaviour and nearness to God over worldly gains and material benefits. Unlike materialists, they ever seek the inner spiritual satisfaction, even if it means renouncing earthly power, honour and riches. This is the moral drawn by Sūrat al-Kahf as well as the lesson taught by the Qur'an.

"And strain not thine eyes toward that which We
cause some wedded pairs among them to enjoy,
the flower of the life of the world, that We may try
them thereby. The provision of thy Lord is better
and more lasting." (Q, 20:131)

Al-Dajjāl and Materialistic Civilization

In reality, Materialistic civilization is the civilization of al-
Dajjāl. It persistently opposes the spirit and a way of life
demanding submission to the Creator and true Master of
the world. Diametrically opposed to the way of Faith and
worship, it issues from the base of worldly gains and rests
on an unbounded admiration for worldly riches and
comfort. Its art and literature, philosophy and thought, are
impregnated with an appalling craze for earthly goods and
benefits, and punctuated with copious praise for those who
hold the reins of economic and political power. It seeks to
endue the objects of human desire with the qualities of
eternity and omnipotence—the very attributes of God—and
to coerce man into dishonourable submission to his own
earthly passions.

Extremism and Exaggeration

The materialist civilization, so prone to over-emphasize it
perspective with extreme measures, has been aptly
described in this verse of Sūrat al-Kahf:

"We have made heedless of Our remembrance, who follows his own lust and whose case has been abandoned." (Q, 18:28)

The dominant traits of this society are reckless exaggerations with ostentatious extravagance and dire extremism. The excessive pursuits of pleasure, sports and amusements, and the extremism in social, economic and political views of materialist camp followers, have made them overconfident absolutists, no matter they be democrats, imperialists, socialists or communists. They cannot brook the slightest deviation from their accepted norms of philosophy or agenda. They reject conclusions which go beyond the limits of their cherished theories as diabolical or reactionary, and dub those who claim freedom of interpreting these concepts as liars. One who does not conform to these extremists forfeits, in their view, the very right to human dignity and respect of life, deserving neither charity nor compassion.[30]

We therefore find its every affair, whether public or private, erring through excess and intemperance. Sobriety,

---

30. In the United States and in many countries of Europe, a new counter-culture is emerging on anarchist principles. The distinguishing features of this new content are moral irresponsibility, mutuality in sex, and nudity of the younger generations, perhaps best represented by the hippies. These trends, in fact, arise from hideous excess of materialism, intellectual unrest, psychic discontent and frustration. We find that almost similar conditions once prevailing in Rome and Greece. The description of the democratic youth given by Plato in his *Republic* is not dissimilar to what obtains in our own times. For details see *Islam and the World*, pages 113-19.

moderation, and restraint are foreign to its overcharged
temperament.

Bases of Revelatory Guidance

The view of life arising from prophetic teachings has equity
and moderation as its two immutable bases. Speaking of the
right-guided persons, the Qur'an says:

> "And those who, when they spend, are neither
> prodigal nor grudging; and there is ever a firm
> station between the two." (Q, 25:67)

Again, the dominant characteristic of the followers of the
Qur'an is stated to be their remarkable moderation:

> "Thus We have appointed you a middle nation,
> that ye may be a witness against mankind, and
> that the Messenger a witness against you." (Q,
> 2:143)

The Prophet himself was an exemplar of absolute and
ennobling moderation.[31] The distinguishing feature of
Islam, described as "the straight path" and "a right
religion", is natural temperance and moderation, refraining
from the aberration of excess or extremism. Addressing the
Prophet of Islam, says God Almighty:

---

31. The biographies of the Prophet of Islam and the compilations of his
Traditions list a number of incidents showing the moderation of his
disposition, the restraint displayed by him in explosive situations, surcharged
with emotion and the temperance of his demeanour. "He always followed the
middle course," says Caliph 'Alī, "Never faltering from the right path, he
always chose the easier course whenever he had two alternatives open to him."
(*Shamā'il al-Tirmidhī*)

"Say: Lo! As for me, my Lord hath guided me unto a straight path, a right religion, the community of Abraham the upright; he was no idolater." (Q, 6:161)

Again, God declares:

"...That is the right religion." (Q, 9:36)

The Qur'an directs on yet another occasion:

"So set thy purpose resolutely for the right religion." (Q, 30:43)

The Qur'an also claims for itself the same characteristic—a clear guidance free from all crookedness. Sūrat al-Kahf begins with the assertion:

"Praise be to Allah Who hath revealed the Scripture unto His slave, and hath not placed therein any crookedness, (but hath made it) straight, to give warning of stern punishment from Him, and to bring unto the believers who do good works the news that theirs will be a fair reward." (Q, 18:1-2)

The same statement is repeated here:

"A messenger from Allah, rehearsing scriptures kept pure and holy." (Q, 98:2-3)

And, again, says God about the Qur'an:

"A Lecture in Arabic, containing no crookedness, that haply they may ward off (evil)." (Q, 39:28)

It cannot be denied therefore, that the spirit of moderation is an undeviating golden mean that runs unswervingly throughout Islam as a guiding principle;

directing its righteous path like a chalked out blueprint that permeates all observances, teachings, guidelines, and cultural patterns. It condemns the extremist tendency arising from the intolerant and mutually exclusive assertions that unfortunately comprise the philosophic pedestal of Western materialism. Materialism has never displayed equilibrium! Its very conception grew from seeds of revolt against religion and morality in Europe during the medieval age; its social philosophies exhibit desperate extremism; its thought and wisdom are erratic; its manners and morals a dump of reckless extravagance; and its constant preference is to adopt the most difficult and crooked course. It is no wonder, then, that this civilization resists all restraints; that it clouds and contradicts fundamental truths; that it abandons simplicity and plainness; and ultimately shuns the fellowship of mutual respect between differing peoples.

III. THE STORY OF THE OWNER OF TWO GARDENS

The second story in this Sūrah relates to a man who owned two gardens. Most of us would have occasionally come across situations espoused by this story. We do not often encounter such bleak conditions faced by the Companions of the Cave, but the story of the owner of two gardens is enacted frequently in every place and age. It is the parable of a man who had made a fortune and possessed the means of necessary comfort. He had two thriving vineyards surrounded by groves of date palms. In between the groves he also had cultivated fields. It was all that a man of middle class means could aspire for; indeed, more than sufficient to lead a happy and contended life. He might not have rolled in riches, but this middle class standard of moderate living has always been the touchstone of prosperity.

Yet the well-being of this man did not depend on his gardens exclusively, for the unseen causes and means required to raise his abundance, had also been put into his service:

"Each of the gardens gave its fruit and withheld naught thereof. And We caused a river to gush forth therein." (Q, 18:33)

67

Thus the owner of the groves thrived on account of a hidden power, bestowed by God and employed as the real causative agent of the man's success and prosperity.

Short-sightedness of the Materialistic View-point

The vision of the owner of two gardens was coloured by the materialism that is almost always entertained by the ruling circles of feudal lords, national leaders, industrialists, and militarists etc. The inherent vigour of this persuasion prevented the owner of the gardens from being enlightened by faith, Divine gnosis, and moral discipline. He ascribed the reason for his prosperity and well-being to his own knowledge and capabilities, intelligence and industry. This was also what Korah once thought of himself.

"He said: I have been given it only on account of knowledge I possess." (Q, 28:78)

The owner of the groves was puffed up by his possessions and large following. This man, pompously exultant, was despising his friend when he said:

"I am more than thee in wealth, and mightier in respect of retinue." (Q, 18:34)

The owner of the groves reaped the benefit of his bountiful crop, and yet was blissfully ignorant of his Lord's benevolence, which was the imperceptible cause contributing to his prosperity, as well as the Will of God Who supervised his weal. Not man, but the Lord and Sustainer of the World has just claim to the possession of whatever exists in the world. He alone is the connecting link between man and his possessions, nay, between his body and soul. Denial of this Divine over-lordship and authority is thus a cruel injustice to one's own self, his understanding, and his intelligence. In fact, this arrogant denial of evident truth concerning God's supreme Lordship, actually fosters the materialistic outlook in man, who then begins to claim unconditional ownership of his possessions, riches, gardens and crops. These insidious thoughts caused him to believe that his possessions, estate or effects, would never be diminished or destroyed, and that the Day of Judgement would never arrive to call him to account. It was, therefore, not at all surprising that the owner of the groves, foolish and unjust to his own soul as he was, thought that his crop would never wither away.

"And he went into his garden, while he (thus) wronged himself. He said: I think not that all this will ever perish. I think not that the 'Hour' will ever come." (Q, 18:35-36)

He thought that he was one of those selected few who were born with a silver spoon in their mouth and whom fate never betrayed nor doom impounded, and who always rolled in riches. He said:

"And if indeed I am brought back unto my Lord, I surely shall find better than this as a resort." (Q, 18:36)

Persons holding such a view have a very high opinion of their own capabilities and gracious fortune. They think that they need not bother about faith and righteousness, or the moral responsibilities entailed thereby, as their affluence is solely due to their merit and not because of any beneficence on the part of God.

Religious Way of Thinking

The friend of this wayward man had been endowed with a sublime faith and was armed with an intuitive knowledge of the 'all-embracing' divine attributes. He knew that God alone is the Maker and Master of the universe, the Cause of all causes with power to alter any situation or circumstance according to His will. He therefore intentionally replied with the responsible suggestion that his friend's materialistic outlook was fallacious. The over-lordship of God is a fundamental and incontrovertible truth, but, and unfortunately, it is also a fact evaded by conceited fellows who disbelieve in the existence of that which is beyond human perception. The very mention of the fact is distasteful to them.

"His comrade, when he (thus) spake with him, exclaimed: Disbelievest thou in Him Who created thee of dust, then of a drop (of seed), and then fashioned thee a man." (Q, 18:37)

One can imagine how unpalatable and annoying such talk was to a purse-proud self-admirer. His friend, however, was a firm believer without any obsession produced by the materialistic outlook. He declared:

"But He is Allah, my Lord, and I ascribe unto My Lord no partner." (Q, 18:38)

The owner of the gardens was then reminded by his friend of the living reality which is the substance of Sūrat al-Kahf. This was a truth, absolute and profound, but also sickening for the spirit of the materialist. He was told that the apparent causes have no importance at all: all power belonged to the Creator and Master of all causes and effects. He was warned that the estate and effects on which he prided rested on hollow foundations; his affluence was neither brought about by the tangible outward causes, nor was it due to his own merit, intelligence, or industry. It was all, in truth and reality, owing to the beneficence of the Wise, Omnipotent Lord, Who has fashioned everything in the best proportion. His attention was thus invited by his comrade toward the imperative need of restoring his faith in the omnipotence and beneficence of the Lord.

> "If only, when thou entered thy garden, thou had
> said: That which Allah wills (will come to pass)
> There is no strength save in Allah."(Q, 18:39)

The Essence of *Sūrat al-Kahf*

'There is no strength save in Allah" carries the essence of *Sūrat al-Kahf*. The Prophet of Islam and every believer reciting the Qur'an has been called upon to place implicit reliance in God in every affair instead of relying on his own resources. Every intention and hope for the morrow has thus to be made dependent on the will and pleasure of God.

> "And say not of anything: Lo! I shall do that
> tomorrow, except if Allah will. And remember thy
> Lord when thou forgettest, and say: It may be that

my Lord guideth me unto a nearer way of truth
than this." (Q, 18:23-24)

If one ascribes every favour to the beneficence of the
Merciful Lord, it is not then possible to bow in submission
before outward material causes, or rely on those who
appear to possess means, nor to submit oneself even to
personal whims, desire, or caprice.

This phrase 'Except if Allah wills' or 'whatsoever
Allah may will', might appear to be commonplace
traditional idiom often repeated mechanically by force of
habit in Islam, but these spoken confessions are very
significant and meaningful *disciplined* expressions of
submission to God's right guidance. They cut at the very
root of ignorant faith in one's own capacity or material
resources, every time they are spoken.

Materialistic Outlook and Material Resources

The materialistic outlook and its 'way of life' that
subsequently arises place absolute reliance on the efficacy
of one's own resources and devices. The plans for social
and economic development that are regularly espoused by
materialistic governments, proclaim from housetops the
production targets that must be achieved within a given
period; irrespective of seasonal variations or the impact of
natural forces.[1] These governments determine the exact

---

1. It does not mean that developmental plans should not be formulated, nor
that efforts to augment production through increased knowledge and skill
should be abandoned. What is meant here is that the increasing human

quantum of production and a definite date by which it has to be realised, often designated as the time within which the country has to achieve *self-sufficiency*, a period, after which, they would not have to rely upon external aid. However, as we often see, natural calamities, such as droughts and floods, forever foil these ambitious plans.

Faith in the Will of God

'Except if God wills' is therefore not an empty customary phrase repeated in daily conversation for fixing up a date or the making of paltry promises. It is really a repetitive drill casting its shadow on the collective life of the entire community! Thereby, it inculcates the habit to pin one's faith in the ultimate and all embracing will of God, despite any and all strenuous effort one might make to achieve the objective. This directive:

> "Nor say of anything, 'I shall be sure to do so and so tomorrow'—without adding, 'So please Allah....'"
> (Q, 18:23-24)

It is not meant for individuals alone! It is an ordinance for the entire community: for governments, for institutions, and for all organisations of believers—and it demands an implicit conviction in the dominant over-lordship of God. Indeed, this is the guiding spirit of the Muslim society, as it draws inspiration from the unflinching conviction in God's

---

knowledge and skill should not give rise to a spirit of revolt against the omnipotent God, Creator of all cause and effects.

Dominion, and the realities beyond the ken of human perception. It also constitutes the line of demarcation between a 'way of life' based on true faith and prophetic guidance, and the 'other way' that arises from an outlook characterised as 'worldly'.

The believing comrade of the owner of two gardens admonished his friend. He informed him that adversity and prosperity, lucky breaks or ill fortunes, were not the abiding or permanent realities of life, *because* the Lord of the world firmly holds the reins of human destiny. God can turn the evil stars of a man into smiles of fortune, or reduce the millionaire to pauperdom in no time. Such changes are not even amazing, as they continually occur. He said:

> "...Though thou seest me as less than thee in wealth and children, yet it may be that my Lord will give me better than thy garden, and will send on it (thy garden) a bolt from heaven, and some morning it will be a smooth hillside, or some morning the water thereof will be lost in the earth so that thou can not make search for it." (Q, 18:39-41)

And this did happen one fine morning. A tearing gale, sent by the Lord, screamed over his groves and swept them away leaving a barren land:

> "And his fruits (and enjoyment) were encompassed (with ruin) and then he remained twisting and turning his hands over what he had spent on his property which had (now) tumbled to

pieces to its very foundations, and he could only say, 'Woe is me! Would I had never ascribed partners to my Lord and Cherisher'. Nor had he numbers to help him against God, nor was he able to deliver himself. There the only protection comes from God, the True One. He is the best to reward, and the best to give success." (Q, 18:42-44)

Impiety of the Owner of the Two Gardens

The owner of the two gardens was neither a heathen nor an agnostic fellow like many other irreligious persons. Nothing in the Qur'an indicates his godlessness. On the contrary, it appears from what is related of him that he professed faith in God. He is reported to have said:

"And if indeed I am brought back unto my Lord I surely shall find (there) something better in exchange." (Q, 18:36)

Then, what was it that he regretted later on?

"Would I had never ascribed partners to my Lord and Cherisher." (Q, 18:42)

Irreligiousness of the Modern Age

This is, in fact, the irreligious association of partners with God, and is the bane of the modern materialistic civilization! It elevates natural resources, technological contrivances, and professional expertise to the level of God. Man has today pinned his hope in material objects and thrown himself on the mercy of specialists and experts. The success and failure, prosperity and adversity, honour and infamy, life and death of the nations, have now been committed to the care of one expert or the other. The arrogant spirit of extreme phenomenalism, the worshipful reverence of brute matter and physical forces along with an overweening confidence in experts, scientists, and technologists, is the new form of irreligiousness. Invested with halos that make them partners of God, these sharers of Divinity are the new gods of a modern age: the latest addition to a myriad pantheon of gods and goddesses. It is this paganism, the polytheism of yore and now of the modern age, which has been challenged by Sūrat al-Kahf.

> "And coin for them the similitude of the life of the world as water: it is like the water We send down from the sky, and the earth's vegetation absorbs it, but soon it becomes dry twigs that the winds do scatter. It is only God Who prevails over all things." (Q, 18:45)

The life of the world is ephemeral. Its fleeting nature is figured by the Qur'an elsewhere—as a fading dream:

> "The similitude of the life of the world is only as water which We send down from the sky, then the earth's growth of that which men and cattle eat mingleth with it till, when the earth hath taken on her ornaments and is embellished, and her people deem that they are masters of her, Our commandment cometh by night or by day and We make it as reaped corns as if it had not flourished

yesterday. Thus do We expound the revelations for
people who reflect." (Q, 10:24)

This is the Qur'anic view of the brief and uncertain life
of this world, an existence generally regarded as durable
and imperishable by the materialists, utilitarians, and
epicureans. The Qur'an repudiates all of these speculative
and fictitious values which have led men to become
worshippers of outer forms and objects, and thus to regard
ease and comfort as the be-all and end-all of the worldly
life. The Qur'an explicitly attaches worth only to the lasting
values that are determined by transcendental truth as
embodied in the revelatory guidance.

"Wealth and children are an ornament of the life
of the world. But the good deeds which endure are
better in thy Lord's sight for reward, and better in
respect of hope." (Q, 18:46)

Qur'an and the Life of the World

Before we proceed further let us spell out the Qur'an's
view of the life of this world. However, since widely
divergent views are advanced in this regard, it would be
advisable to take cognizance of the Qur'anic statements
only. The Qur'an vehemently proclaims the transitory and
perishable nature of worldly life to be an abject
insignificance when compared to the eternal life of the
Hereafter. It says:

"The comfort of the life of the world is but little in
the Hereafter." (Q, 9:38)

At another place it declares:

> "Know that the life of the world is only play, and
> idle talk, and pageantry, and boasting among you,
> and rivalry in respect of wealth and children; as the
> likeness of vegetation after rain, whereof the
> growth is pleasing to the husbandman, but
> afterward it drieth up and thou seest it turning
> yellow, then it becometh straw. And in the
> Hereafter there is grievous punishment, and (also)
> forgiveness from Allah and His good pleasure,
> whereas the life of the world is but matter of
> illusion." (Q, 57:20)

The life of the world is but a bridge we must all cross
over to the Hereafter. It is a means to test a man's qualities:

> "Lo ! We have placed all that is in the earth as an
> ornament thereof that We may try them: which of
> them is best in conduct." (Q, 18:7)

Again it says:

> "Who hath created life and death that He may try
> you, which of you is best in conduct; and He is the
> Mighty, the Forgiving." (Q, 67:2)

And it holds the life of the Hereafter *alone*, as abiding
and eternal:

> "Naught is the life of the world save a pastime and
> a sport. Better far is the abode of the Hereafter for
> those who keep their duty (to Allah). Have ye then
> no sense." (Q, 6:32)

The same view is expounded in Sūrat al-Qaṣaṣ:

"And whatsoever ye have been given is a comfort of the life of the world and an ornament thereof; and that which Allah hath is better and more lasting. Have ye then no sense?" (Q, 28:60)

The Qur'an severely condemns those who prefer the ephemeral, mortal and insignificant life of the world, to the abiding, eternal and marvellous life in the Hereafter:

"Lo! Those who expect not the meeting with Us but desire the life of the world and feel secure therein, and those who are neglectful of Our revelations, their home will be the Fire because of what they used to earn." (Q, 10:7-8)

The same warning is repeated elsewhere:

"Whoso desireth the life of the world and its pomp, We shall repay them their deeds herein, and therein they will not be wronged. Those are they for whom is naught in the Hereafter save the Fire. (All) that they contrive here is vain and (all) that they are wont to do is fruitless." (Q, 11:15-16)

In Sūrat Ibrāhīm it says:

"And woe unto the disbelievers from an awful doom; those who love the life of the world more than the Hereafter, and debar (men) from the way of Allah and would have it crooked: such are far astray." (Q, 14:2-3)

And, again:

"They know only some appearance of the life of the world, and are heedless of the Hereafter." (Q, 30:7)

The Prophet is advised thus in Sūrat al-Najm:

> "Then withdraw (O Muhammad) from him who flees from Our remembrance and desires but the life of the world. Such is their sum of knowledge. Lo! Thy Lord is Best Aware of him who strays, and He is Best Aware of him who goes right." (Q, 53:29-30)

It reminds of the short-sightedness of such persons:

> "Lo! They love fleeting life, and put behind them (the remembrance of) a grievous day." (Q, 76:27)

> "Then, as for him who rebelled, and chose the life of world, Lo! Hell will be his home." (Q, 79:37-39)

The Qur'an lauds such persons who combine the blessings of this world with those of the next, but give preference to the Hereafter over their earthly sojourn:

> "But of mankind is he who says: 'Our Lord! Give unto us in the world,' and he hath no portion in the Hereafter. And of them (also) is he who says: 'Our Lord! Give unto us in the world that which is good and in the Hereafter that which is good, and guard us from the doom of Fire'." (Q, 2:200-201)

It quotes the prayer offered by Prophet Moses:

> "And ordain for us in this world that which is good, and in the Hereafter (that which is good)." (Q, 7:156)

Praising Abraham, God says:

> "And We gave him good in the world, and in the Hereafter he is among the righteous." (Q, 16:122)

Revelatory and Materialistic Views of Life

The view of life and the world order as enunciated by the prophetic teachings of revelatory guidance thus vouchsafed to man are diametrically opposed to that put forth by the materialistic attitude that assigns supreme importance to terrestrial life, and whose constant aim is to achieve worldly power, glory, wealth, position, comfort, and all that gratify man's longings and appetites.

The sayings of the blessed Prophet clearly expound the Qur'anic view of life. The Prophet often used to say:

"O Allah, life is only that of the Hereafter."[2]

He used to beseech God:

"O Allah, provide for the progeny of Muhammad only that which is essential."[3]

Mustawrad ibn Shaddād relates that he heard the Prophet saying:

"By God, the life of the world in comparison to Hereafter is no more than the water left on a finger dipped in the ocean."[4]

The life of the Prophet was the ideal embodiment of his teachings and the outlook of life arising therefrom. Ibn Mas'ūd relates that once the Prophet was lying on a mat, whose marks were visible on his body. He (Ibn Mas'ūd) said: "If you permit, I may spread something on it." "What

---

2. *Ṣaḥīḥ al-Bukhārī, Kitāb al-Raqāq.*
3. *Ṣaḥīḥ Muslim, Kitāb al-Zuhd.*
4. *Ṣaḥīḥ Muslim.*

have I to do with the world," replied the Prophet, "for me it
is like a shady tree under which a traveller takes rest for a
while and then leaves on his errand."[5]

In a Tradition, Caliph 'Umar narrates:

> "Once I went to the Prophet when he was lying on
> a mat without a bedding or a bed-sheet. The pillow
> on which he was leaning was made of leather
> stuffed with straw, and the crossed pattern of the
> matting could easily be seen imprinted on his
> body. I saluted the Prophet... I cast a glance over
> the house. By God there was nothing which I saw
> except three pieces of leather. I said, 'O Prophet,
> Pray God to bless your followers with abundance.
> The Persians and the Romans have been favoured
> with all the pleasures of the world, although they
> believe not in Allah! Startled to hear this, the
> Prophet got up and said, 'Ibn al-Khaṭṭāb, you too
> think like this! These are the fellows who have got
> all their rewards in the comforts of this world
> alone.'"[6]

Behaviour of the Prophet's Companions

The care of Hereafter got enshrined in the heart of those
who had the good fortune of being put through the mill of
prophetic guidance. It became their guiding star, their

---

5. *Aḥmad, al-Tirmidhī and Ibn Mājah.*
6. *Ṣaḥīḥ al-Bukhārī, Kitāb al-Nikāḥ.*

greatest yearning, and the culmination of their pious desires. They were never negligent of its demands for a moment, nor were they willing to accept anything in its place. In order to have a glimpse of the spirit of the "other-worldliness", this posture and bent of mind, common to all the companions of the Prophet of Islam, it would suffice us to have a look at the character and demeanour of Caliph 'Alī. His life was a striking example of the piety, simplicity, godliness, and other sterling qualities fashioned by the benevolent care of the Prophet in his followers and companions.

Abū Ṣāliḥ has given a graphic description of Caliph 'Alī's character. He says that once, Caliph Mu'āwiyah asked Ḍirār ibn Ḍamurah, a companion of Caliph 'Alī ibn abī Ṭālib, to narrate something about the latter. Ḍirār first asked to be excused but when Caliph Mu'āwiyah insisted on it, he said:

> "All right, then listen to me. He ('Alī) was farsighted and strong and possessed a robust health. He always spoke what was true and dispensed impartial justice. He was like a fountain of knowledge or a repository of wisdom. Being always scared of the world and its pleasures, the night and its darkness were pleasing to him. By God, his eyes were more often brimming with tears and he always appeared to be care-worn. He liked to wear garments made of rough cloth and to partake in coarse food, lived like a commoner, and

made no distinction between himself and others.
Whenever we asked him anything, he would
answer; whenever we went to him, he would salute
first; and whenever we invited him, he would
come ungrudging but, despite his nearness, his awe
never permitted us to talk in his presence or join in
his conversation. He respected the pious and loved
the poor; the powerful could never hope to achieve
any undeserved gain from him; nor did the weak
ever give up hope obtaining justice from him. By
God, I have seen him often after the night-fall
standing on his prayer-mat, holding his beard and
weeping as if he were bitten by a snake. Often in the
dead of night, he could be heard asking the world to
leave him alone and give up all hopes of enticing
him away to its pleasures. I could still visualise him
saying thus: 'O World, thy pleasures are transitory,
thy life short, thy allurements unreliable and
dangerous while I have to cover an arduous, long,
and extremely perilous path'."[7]

Now, here is another example reflecting the spirit of
the same philosophy of life. It is an extract from the address
delivered by a companion of the Prophet in the then
metropolis of Islam. Khālid ibn 'Umayr al-'Adawiy relates
that 'Utbah ibn Ghazwān, the then governor of Basrah,
addressed a congregation as follows:

---

7. Ibn al-Jawzī: Ṣafwat al-Ṣafwah, Hyderabad, 1935, vol.I, p.122.

"Verily, the world is nearing its end; running out fast to its doom, it has now only a few drops of nectar in its cup to offer you. You are about to migrate to a place where you would have to live forever; therefore set out for it with the provisions of virtue and goodness. We have been told that a stone would be thrown in Hell but it would not reach its bottom even in seventy years, and, by God, this vast place of torment would ultimately be filled with the wrong-doers. Do you have any doubt about it? We have been told that the two corners of the Heaven's threshold would lie at a distance of forty year's journey, but it would also be overcrowded one day. I still remember the days when we had nothing to eat except leaves of the trees for weeks together, and our mouths bled because of it. Once I got a bed-sheet which I had to divide into two, one for myself and the other I gave to Sa'īd ibn Mālik. Now, every one of us is a governor of one city or the other, but I seek refuge in God from assigning any merit to my own self while I am really insignificant in the eyes of Lord."[8]

Modern Apologists of the Hereafter

Those persons who are not inspired by the prophetic teachings, and those not endowed with sincere faith, find it

---

8. *Ṣaḥīḥ Muslim*, vol.II, *Kitāb al-Zuhd*.

difficult to accept the Life-After-Death or the Day of
Judgement and Retribution with a deep conviction. On the
contrary, and being shaken by the very concept of an
after-life, their interest, if any, is always distracted and
desultory. They essentially lack the 'warmth of heart' for
the Life-After-Death. This 'warmth' is a distinguishing
feature of the Prophet's followers and all revealed
guidance. These apologists are escapists by nature; always
trying to explain away the life-to-come through subtle
sophistry. They look upon the concept of the Hereafter as
no more than a figurative expression meant for the bygone
days of primitive intelligence, when it was designed as an
expedient for righteous action.

But it is a striking and incontrovertible fact that the
Qur'an and its teachings, as well as the life of the Prophet
of Islam, are both permeated with the spirit of Life-After-
Death. This is the mindset that prophetic guidance seeks to
build in its followers. Therefore we find this distinctive
inclination—this bent of mind and predisposition—in all
truly Islamic societies which are brought up in accordance
with an Islamic Doctrine that is kept free from extraneous
contamination.

Showing least concern for the worldly pleasures and
possessions; being pleasantly temperate in behaviour;
anxious for the Hereafter with its ultimate sequel;
commanding piety and virtue; preferring that which is
promised in the after-life over earthly power and pelf;
overflowing with the desire to court death and meet their

Lord; of such are the distinctive characteristics of true believers whose eagerness for nearness to God finds its penultimate expression in the solemn yearning of Bilāl:

"Tomorrow shall I meet my favourites and friends,
Muhammad, on whom be peace and blessings of
God, and his companions."[9]

Prophetic Call and Reformatory Movements

There are also revivalist and reformatory movements which expound the concept of the Hereafter. Along with its underlying wisdom and benefits that accordingly flow from its inspiration, the invaluable contribution of this concept to establishing a stable society that is imbued with the sense of moral responsibility is inestimable. But, evidently, the philosophy of after-life is often employed solely as a means of educating the people, in order to impress upon them the spiritual-moral view of life preached by Islam. There is no denying the fact that their endeavour is praise-worthy, for one cannot have a congenial, orderly, and ethical society without inculcating the belief in the Hereafter. At the same time, however, the method adopted by these movements is quite different from the way of thought, the procedure of reform, and the behaviour and deportment of the prophets and their followers.

The methodology of reform evolved by God's apostles is inspired by an unflinching faith and sincere conviction in

---

9. *Iḥyā' al-'Ulūm*, on the authority of Ibn Abī al-Dunyā.

the After-Life; it is a living faith which encompasses the entire being of the believer. Unfortunately, the reformist movements are simply an external or outward expression of these deep-seated emotions of faith. The discourses of the former on the sequel and Life-After-Death are marked by their instinctive conviction, while the latter promote the idea only as an expedient to social and moral reform of the people hoping that will raise up a coherent, stable and ethical society. The difference between logical disputations and secret springs of conviction, and the results achieved by the two schools, are too well known to be discussed here in any detail.

The Mainspring of Courage and Zeal

The unshakable belief of the Prophet of Islam and his companions in the Life-After-Death, and their unconditional preference to its rewards over the earthly pleasures of the world, did not induce them to cut themselves adrift from the mainstream of life, nor to relinquish its leadership. It never occurred to them that they should give up their means of livelihood or abandon their struggle for faith, justice and righteousness. Their faith was not a product of disheartened defeatism, as we find today among certain people.

On the contrary, it was a fountainhead of valour and courage that inspired them to fight evil until virtue and goodness were victorious. It is, therefore, not at all surprising that those who were the most virtuous and had the most intense conviction in God and in the after-life, were also those who despised the earthly pleasures and intensely desired closeness to God in the Hereafter—these were also the most courageous, brave and valiant fighters in the way of God. Theirs was, in fact, the greatest contribution in the lightning success of Islam in its early phases!

Disdainfulness of earthly possessions and pleasures, self-restraint over one's longings and passions, valiant and courageous defiance of the evil, and similar other ennobling qualities are the end-product of a person's conviction in the eternal Life-After-Death. The conquests achieved by the sword-arm of Islam, and the diffusion of this religion in far-off lands at the hands of serene preachers of the faith, owed their success to the firm conviction in the Resurrection and Retribution in the Life-After-Death.

Monasticism and the Belief in Hereafter

The belief in the Hereafter, as expounded by the Qur'an, has little to do with the rightly despised monastic life: celibacy and asceticism. The latter has been firmly condemned by the Qur'an, although it gained ground among the Muslims later on due to negligence of Islamic doctrine and interaction with extraneous encouragements from Christianity, Buddhism, Brahmanism, and Neo-Platonism.

Belief in the Hereafter commands the deliberate choice of itself, and without denying or denigrating the just and inescapable demands of earthly life. It encourages us to engage in the unending contest for the victory of righteousness, to sacrifice fleeting desires for the eternal life-to-come, and to lay down our lives 'in the way' or 'cause' of our Lord and Master. There is not the least doubt that Muslims have been rendered weak solely because of the weakening of their devotion to the Hereafter. The younger generations of the Muslims today are the unhappy victims of their own longings and desires, and need the healing faith in the after-life more than anyone else, in order to recover their lost vitality.

Muslims will not regain their strength again, nor will their faith be complete, until they endorse the Qur'anic philosophy of life. Sadly, this view of life and the world is violently opposed by the modern materialistic outlook. On the other hand, those persons who have been enchanted by the materialist perspective would not agree to anything short of worldly ease and comfort, the fulfilment of their base desires, or the power, position and glory of the transitory life of the world. Sūrat al-Kahf exposes the weakness of the materialistic outlook on life, its hollow promise as endorsed by its votaries, and pronounces a constant and bitter reproach intended for its disciples. It presents life in true focus, no matter if certain people like it or not.

IV. THE STORY OF MOSES AND AL-KHIḌR

Now we turn to the story of Moses and al-Khiḍr. It is in reality the story of everyday life, wherein, often we come across paradoxical situations that draw our attention to the fact that there remain numbers of inexplicable things beyond the sphere of our knowledge. These incidents tell us that howsoever learned a man might be the decisions, estimates and opinions, formed on the basis of his still limited knowledge and experience, sometimes go astray. If the secrets of life were, somehow, made known to someone, we would undoubtedly find a visible change in his ideas, modes of thought and decisions.

This episode in the life of Moses is also meant to illustrate that one can never be dead sure of opinions formed or impressions gained, and that neither should one take a stand on the basis of ephemeral knowledge. It demonstrates that it is rather impossible for human knowledge to comprehend and cover the totality of universal knowledge, and, therefore, one should not be hasty in arriving at conclusions, nor should one insist on the acceptance of his opinions and impressions by others.

Life is itself a parable—secretive, variable, and uncertain. The universe is much too wide and incomprehensible, with secrets and complexities that

91

clearly stand apart from the external, outer realities. These
often present us with paradoxes that are unsolvable by man
despite his constant quest for knowledge. In fact, there are
numerous mysteries of nature we might never be able to
unravel, despite all the scientific inventions and discoveries
at our command. Even in our mundane life of day-to-day
affairs, we are confronted with many a complex situation
created by mistakes and half-baked ideas, or our hasty
decisions and immature emotional behaviours.

Now, if man were to be entrusted with the governance
of this vast and complex universe, with a free hand to do
whatever he likes, he would soon fill it with strife and
trouble, and no doubt take it to the brink of total
destruction. This would simply be because of his limited
knowledge, which is unfortunately, also conditioned by his
predisposition to hasty action.

In order to demonstrate the limitation of human
knowledge, which also forms the basis of faith in unseen
realities, God selected one of the greatest prophets, Moses,
who had been endowed with knowledge, virtue, and piety.
Moses once stood preaching to his people, when he was
asked whether he knew of a man who was wiser than him
Moses answered in the negative. Not pleased by the reply
of Moses, who ought to have ascribed his knowledge to
God alone, he was directed to meet a man more knowing
than himself at a place where the two seas met.[1]

---

1. *Ṣaḥīḥ al-Bukhārī*, vol III; *Kitāb al-Tafsīr*.

Strange and Bewildering Events

Moses set out on the journey with a companion, to find the man who had been endowed with a special knowledge not granted to ordinary mortals. We will presently see that the special knowledge granted to this man of God did come into conflict with the human knowledge based on experiences and apparent situations.

Al-Khiḍr boards a boat whose owner does not charge the fare for him and on reaching his destination, al-Khiḍr knocks out a few of her planks. Moses, not understanding the import of al-Khiḍr's action, rebukes and asks him to explain what he has done. Next, al-Khiḍr kills an innocent youth: a boy who had done him no harm; neither had the child's parents been a source of anxiety to him. At another place, al-Khiḍr helps in the repair of a dilapidated wall although the inhabitants of the place had been inhospitable to him. These were undoubtedly strange and weird incidents that raised a storm of curiosity in the heart of Moses.

These inexplicable events, naturally, prompted him to ask al-Khiḍr to explain why he had scuttled the boat which had taken them to the shore safely. It ought to have been protected and not broken. The owner of the boat, too, deserved thanks from al-Khiḍr rather than his enmity. The innocent boy ought to have been received with kindness, and looked after instead of being put to death. Similarly, the inhabitants of the village who had been so unkind and unsocial were entitled to a stern behaviour. Al-Khiḍr, however, appears to be taking decisions not commanded by

wisdom or outwardly known facts—judgements certainly
not warranted by emotions and instincts.

Moses was, after all, a prophet of God, endowed with
faith and a kind heart, and therefore could not tolerate the
flagrant acts of apparent injustice committed by his
comrade. He forgot the promise he made at the start of the
journey, to ask no question about anything, that is, until al-
Khiḍr himself explained it to him. Accordingly and
impatiently he exclaimed:

"Verily thou hast done a horrid thing." (Q, 18:74)

Al-Khiḍr gives no reply to the questions and goes on to
complete the mission for which they had undertaken the
journey. At last, having arrived at their destination, al-
Khiḍr reveals the mysteries that Moses found inexplicably
bewildering. Anyone who goes through the Qur'an would
see that al-Khiḍr was right. Whatever he did was not only
correct and logical in the given circumstances, but it also
unfolded practical wisdom. He did not take a wrong
decision on any of the three occasions.

He took out a plank or two from the boat in order to
make it unseaworthy and thus saved it from seizure. The
fact was that the unjust king of that land seized on every
boat he could get in a serviceable condition. The owner of
the boat had not charged any fare from al-Khiḍr, so the
latter repaid the courtesy of the boatman by saving his boat
from seizure.

The boy slain by al-Khiḍr was to become a source of
grief and danger to the faith of his parents. He would have

grown as an infidel and led his parents to renounce their faith out of their excessive fondness for him. Al-Khiḍr thought it preferable that the parents of the boy should better come to grief on account of the boy's death in this life, rather than suffer eternal torments of the Hereafter. Another son could be had if this one died, but nothing could be had in return for a life of unbelief or an evil death:

"And as for the lad, his parents were believers and we feared lest he should oppress them by rebellion and disbelief. And we intended that their Lord should change him for them for one better in purity and nearer to mercy." (Q, 18:80-81)

The wall was in a ruinous state. If it had fallen, the treasure concealed beneath it and owned by two orphan boys, would have been exposed. It would have then been despoiled by the selfish people of the town and the orphan boys would not have got anything of their rightful patrimony. This also illustrates that virtuous action benefits a man after his death as much as during his life-time. Obviously, if God does not like to ignore the progeny of a righteous man after his death, He would certainly not forsake one who is upright and guiltless.

"Allah loses not the wages of the kindly." (Q, 12:90)

"And their Lord has heard them (and He says): Lo! I suffer not the work of any worker, male or female, to be lost." (Q, 3:195)

Verily, Allah gives a fair return of whatever we do.

"And as for the wall, it belonged to two orphan
boys in the city, and there was beneath it a treasure
belonging to them, and their father had been
righteous, and thy Lord intended that they should
come to their full strength and should bring forth
their treasure as a mercy from their Lord; and I did
it not upon my own command. Such is the
interpretation of that wherewith you could not
bear." (Q, 18:82)

Limitations of Human Knowledge

The realities of things are very often so different from what
they appear to us according to our imperfect lights. The
interior of a thing differs from its exterior—the outer form
from the inside reality—how much of life is and remains
mysterious and unpredictable? And how incomprehensible
and enigmatic are the secrets of the Universe? But man is
hotheaded enough to claim that his knowledge can compass
all: the secrets of man as well as of universe, even down to
their core and inner-most realities! At first sight al-Khiḍr
appeared to depart from apparent realities and his actions
bore the look of senselessness. But, to the end of the
chapter, we find that he acted realistically—with wisdom!
The story illustrates that life is ever on the move,
presenting us with situations and new realities from its
inexhaustible store of secrets and mysteries in every age.
The episode also elucidates that knowledge is limitless, and
far beyond the scope of human comprehension.

"... and over all endued with knowledge is One the
All-Knowing." (Q, 12:76)

A Challenge to Materialistic Outlook

The story narrated here is a challenge to the materialistic
way of thought. Materialism claims that life is nothing
more than what is explicable; that it possesses the secrets of
nature and universe; and only that is to be believed is
tangible and capable of being comprehended by human
perception. Therefore, that which is perceptible is the only
reality, and the rest is non-existent, visionary, and
obviously baseless. Furthermore, the materialist claims that
man is the rightful owner and master of this world.
Materialism elevates man to the position of lawgiver,
claims perfection for human knowledge, and assumes that
nothing in this vast and complex universe is beyond human
comprehension.

These have always been the fundamental postulates of
materialistic thought, and so it is today. Sūrat al-Kahf in
general and the episode of Moses in particular, strike at the
root of materialistic thought. The story concludes with
these words of al-Khiḍr:

"Such is the interpretation of that wherewith you
could not bear." (Q, 18:82)

Interpretation signifies, in the phraseology of the
Qur'an, the explanation of a reality.[2] Man is always

---

2. Vide Commentary of Sūrat al-Ikhlāṣ by Ibn Taymiyyah.

predisposed to commit mistakes by taking hasty decisions then rashly deny the existence of a Reality; but when he is confronted with truth and stubborn facts, he has ultimately to accept the realities of situation.

The fourth and the last story narrated in Sūrat al-Kahf, relates to a man who had not only been favoured with a solemn faith but had also at his command power and glory, stupendous assets, and natural resources. This man directed his energies to humble the cruel tyrants of his day for the benefit of suffering humanity, and to establish a just, humane, and civilized order of society.

V. DHŪ AL-QARNAYN

Identification of Dhū al-Qarnayn

The commentators of the Qur'an hold divergent opinions about Dhū al-Qarnayn. Many suppose the person to be Alexander the Great. Imām al-Rāzī is of this, view along with the majority of commentators, but actually, there is no valid reason to accept this opinion. Alexander the Great lacked most of the characteristics and achievements of Dhū al-Qarnayn that have been expressly mentioned in the Qur'an; for example, faith in the One and Only God, piety, just treatment to conquered people, and the erection of an iron rampart. Perhaps the identification of Dhū al-Qarnayn with Alexander the Great was due to the imperfect details of his character and exploits then available to the earlier commentators.

There are, however, other doctors of religion who identify Dhū al-Qarnayn with the Iranian Emperor Cyrus, known to Jews as the Redeemer of Israel, and to Arabs by the name of Kaikhusroe.[1] But the view expressed by Sayyid

---

1. This is the view put forth in some detail by Abul Kalām Āzād, in Volume II of the *Tarjumān al-Qur'ān*, wherein he has adduced numerous references from historical treatises and Jewish religious records in support of his thesis. A summary of it is given here. A remarkable personality came to the fore in a dramatic manner in 559 B. C., and soon attracted the attention of the whole

world. Persia was then divided into two kingdoms: the southern part was known as Persia and the north-western portion was called Media (Arabs called it Mahat). Cyrus welded the Persian tribes into a single nation by defeating Astyages of Media at Pasargadae. Thereafter began the conquests of Cyrus which were marked not by sanguine battles and cruelties, but with humanity and mildness to the vanquished inhabitants and honour to the defeated monarchs. Within 12 years, all the lands from the Black Sea to Bactria had been reduced to the position of Persian dependencies.

In the spring of 546 B.C. Croesus of Lydia attacked Persia; Cyrus flung himself upon him, beat him at Ptgeria in Cappadocia, and pursued him to Lydia, the Northwestern part of Asia Minor, which was then the centre of Hellenistic civilization in Asia.

A second victory followed on the banks of Pactolus: by the autumn of 546 B.C. Sardis had already fallen, and the Persian forces advanced to the Mediterranean. During the next few years the Greek littoral towns were reduced. In 539 B.C. Nabonidus was defeated and Babylon occupied, which, with the Chaldean Empire, Syria and Palestine, also became Persian.

When Cyrus would have advanced beyond Sardis he must have turned back from the coast of the Aegean Sea, near Smyrna. Here he would have seen the sea taking the shape of a lake and the sun setting in murky water: 'he found it setting in muddy spring,' as the Qur'an puts it. (18:86).

In his eastward expedition, Cyrus conquered the lands up to Makran and Balkh. In this region he subdued the uncivilized nomadic tribes, which have also been referred to in the Qur'an: 'he found it (sun) rising on a people for whom We had appointed no shelter there from'. (18:90)." After reducing Babylon, Cyrus rescued the Jews from the tyranny of Nabonidus, as predicted in the Jewish scriptures. He permitted the Jews in Babylon to return to rebuild Jerusalem.

The last campaign of Cyrus was in the direction of the lands despoiled by the people called Gog and Magog. Cyrus advanced towards the Caucasus, leaving Caspian Sea to his right, where he came across a mountain pass between two steep hills rising like walls. Here he constructed the iron rampart to check the ingress of Gog and Magog.

Cyrus met his end in 529 B.C. A marble statute with two horns on his head, signifying the unified kingdoms of Persia and Media, was recovered from the ruins of Pasargadae in 1938. The unification of these two kingdoms gave Cyrus the title of Dhū al-Qarnayn. Cyrus has been rightly praised by most of the modern historians for his conquests as well for his just and mild treatment

Quṭub in *Fī Ẓilāl al-Qur'ān*, appears to us more logical than the explanations given by other commentators:

"The Qur'an does not specify the identity or the time and place of Dhū al-Qarnayn. This is a style of narration peculiar to the stories mentioned in the Qur'an, for its aim is not to historicise the events but to draw out the moral and lesson of the story. The purpose can very often be achieved without determining the location and chronology of the events mentioned in the Qur'an.

"Our recorded history does mention an emperor by the name of Alexander Dhū al-Qarnayn[2] but it is certain that he was not the personality meant by the Qur'an. Alexander the Great was polytheist and an idol worshipper, while the sovereign mentioned in the Qur'an was a man of God, a Unitarian, having faith in the Day of Judgement, Resurrection, etc.

"In his book entitled *Al-Athār al-Bāqiyah 'an al-Qurūn al-Khāliyah*, Abū Rayhān al-Bīrūnī writes that Dhū al-Qarnayn spoken of in the Qur'an belonged to Hymar[3] as the name itself indicates. The Kings of Hymar had *Dhū* as an essential part of their names; as e.g., Dhū Nuwās, Dhū Yazān.

---

of the conquered people (For further details see *Universal History of the World*, vol.II, by J.A. Hammerton).

2. Literally "The two horned" one.

3. An ancient South Arabian people.

The proper name of Dhū al-Qarnayn was Abū
Bakr ibn Afriqash. He subdued all the lands on the
coast of the Mediterranean Sea; including Tunis
and Morocco, and founded a city called Afriqiah
which gave its name to the entire continent. He
was called by the name of Dhū al-Qarnayn as he
was believed to have reached the lands of rising
and setting sun.

"This view might be correct but we have no
means to verify it. The extant records of history
hardly contain anything about him, and the
description of his character and conquests given in
the Qur'an is too general like that of the peoples of
Noah, Hūd, Ṣāliḥ, etc. Actually the records
preserved by our history constitute only a fraction
of our life-story on this earth. We have no record
of the events that took place before history began
to list them. Its verdict is thus not at all reliable.

"If only the Old Testament could have been
preserved in its pristine purity, without inter-
polations and additions, it could have served as a
valuable source of history. But, unfortunately,
numerous legends have been introduced and
interwoven with the revelation contained in this
Scripture, with the result that the historical events
mentioned in it cannot be relied upon.

"The Qur'an being free from all additions,
alterations and mutilation, can, undoubtedly, be a

trustworthy source of the events narrated by it, but its version cannot, obviously, be verified from the historical records. This is so because of two reasons: first, the history does not account for innumerable happenings, and secondly, the Qur'an unfolds some of those events of the olden times which have not been recorded at all.

"There is another reason too: Recorded history, even if it contains the details of any particular happening, is, after all, a human endeavour always *liable to* mistakes or misrepresentation of the event in question. With all the facilities of communications, means of transmitting news and the techniques of their verification in the modern times, we sometimes come across different versions of one and the same story. The same event is not less often interpreted differently, viewed from different angles and widely differing conclusions are drawn there-from. This is, in truth, the basic material which serves as the source of history: it is, however, an entirely different matter that we devise elaborate norms for post-scrutiny and verification of the authenticity of the material so collected.

"Therefore, it is against the accepted principles of literary criticism, as well as Qur'anic exegesis, to seek historical evidence for the verification of events related by the Qur'an. Moreover, this procedure is also not in accord with the conviction which claims to profess the Qur'an as the eternal, unchangeable word of God. Absolute reliance cannot, obviously, be placed on the data thus collected by history either by one having faith in the revelatory nature of the Qur'an or by an impartial literary critic. Historical data is, at best, no more than a collection of our impressions, estimates, and ideas about the past happenings.

"The Prophet had been asked about Dhū al-Qarnayn. Thereupon God revealed certain salient characteristics of the monarch known by that name. Now, the Qur'an being the only source of knowledge about him, the verification of its historicity or otherwise is beyond our means. The commentaries of the Qur'an present differing views in the matter and therefore, reliance cannot be placed on them. If any particular view is endorsed by any commentator, he ought to be extremely cautious for numerous traditions of yore and Israelite legends have found their way into some of the old commentaries."[4]

It hardly makes any difference to a student of the Qur'an whether he is able to identify Dhū al-Qarnayn with any sovereign in the light of available historical records or not. It should be sufficient for him that the Qur'an has

---

4. *Fī Zilāl al-Qur'ān*, Volume VI (V Edition) pp. 8-10.

indicated the dominant characteristics of Dhū al-Qarnayn. We know that he was endowed with political and military power, manifold resources, courage, large heartedness, and nobility of character.

> "Verily We! We established him in the earth, and vouchsafed unto him of everything a way (to attain anything he desired). Then he followed a way." (Q, 18:84-85)

Conquests of Dhū al-Qarnayn

The conquests of Dhū al-Qarnayn were quite extensive. His campaigns were directed to far-off lands in the eastern and western directions which have been alluded to in the Qur'an as the rising place and the setting place of the sun. He conducted his wars with great humanity, administered his subjects mildly, looked after the weak and the poor with loving care, and dealt with the insolent and bully in a stringent manner. The organisation of his empire was planned throughout on the lines indicated by the Qur'an.

> "He said: As for him who doeth wrong, we shall punish him, and then he will be brought back unto his Lord, Who will punish him with awful punishment! But as for him who believeth and doeth right, good will be his reward, and We shall speak unto him a mild command." (Q, 18:87-88)

Mark the distinctive features of the state policy indicated by Dhū al-Qarnayn: it speaks volumes of his judiciousness, moderation, and sagacity as well as nobility of character. During his campaigns, Dhū al-Qarnayn found a people settled between the two hills that were continuously harassed and attacked by the nomadic tribes from across the hills. The Qur'an as well as other scriptures names these tribes as Yājūj and Mājūj (Gog and Magog).[5] The turbulent tribes continuously raided and plundered the land of the other nation.

> "And on that day We shall let some of them surge against others" (Q, 18:99)

Construction of the Iron Rampart

For the weak but peace-loving nation, the arrival of Dhū al-Qarnayn was a God-sent opportunity. They requested the mighty Emperor to protect them from the depredations of the wild and turbulent tribes by erecting a barrier between them and their enemies. They even expressed their willingness to purchase immunity by contributing their

---

5. We entirely agree with the view, reproduced here, expressed by Sayyid Quṭub:

"We cannot definitely indicate the location of the two hills between which Dhū al-Qarnayn had passed through, nor do we know anything else about this place. It appears from the Qur'an that it was a valley between two mountains where had settled a backward and weak people who could not understand the language spoken by Dhū al-Qarnayn (*Fī Ẓilāl al-Qur'ān* vol. XIII, p. 13).

"So far as the matters relating to the identification of Gog and Magog, the destruction of the rampart holding them in check and their pouring forth from their land to plunder and ruin the earth are concerned, one can find lengthy details in the commentaries of the Qur'an and the Traditions, particularly those relating to the advent of the Doomsday. All this material, although by no means extensive, needs careful study and re-interpretation by some one sincerely interested in the task."

mite towards construction of the barrier. Dhū al-Qarnayn accepted their request to get the barrier constructed, but unlike most of the greedy rulers, he did not do so to augment his treasure but to protect his subjects. He did not, therefore, impose too heavy a taxation to meet the cost of proposed construction, but simply required them to provide available labour and material.

"He said: That wherein my Lord hath established me is better (than your tribute). Do but help me with strength (of men), I will set between you and them a bank. Give me pieces of iron... (Q, 18:95-96)

Dhū al-Qarnayn provided the motivational force and the organising skill, while the local population helped with men and material for the construction of the barrier.

. . . till, when he had levelled up (the gap) between the cliffs, he said: Blow!—till, when he had made it a fire, he said: Bring me molten copper to pour thereon." (Q, 18:96)

At last the barrier was completed which afforded protection to that nation against the incursions of the nomads.

"And (Gog and Magog) were not able to surmount, nor could they pierce (it)." (Q, 18:97)

Wisdom Vouchsafed to the Believers

Dhū al-Qarnayn was a mighty emperor and the victor of nations, but his conquests never filled him with conceit. He

never said: I have been given it only on account of
knowledge I possess;[6] on the contrary, he ascribed his
achievements to God. He did not even brag of the
impregnability of the barrier constructed by him. Like a
true believer in God and the Hereafter he laid more stress
on the help and grace of God.

"He said, 'This is a mercy from my Lord; but
when the promise of Lord cometh to pass, He will
lay it low, for the promise of my Lord is true'."
(Q, 18:98)

And this is the attitude of a true believer and a man of
God. He never forgets his Lord—not even when he is
crowned with the most brilliant victories or when he gains
control over gigantic resources and the sinews of earthly
power. He turns his attention to God in the hour of
triumphant success and remembers the ultimate end, when
he would crumble to dust and be raised again; he fearfully
trembles with the awe of God; acknowledges his own
weakness; offers solace and mercy to suffering humanity;
preserves truth and justice; and directs his incessant
endeavour to serve his fellow-beings; creates a just and
virtuous social order; and brings out the ignorant from dark
alleys of godlessness and crass materialism to the sunshine
of divine light and natural religion. This was the noble and
virtuous path trodden by Solomon and Dhū al-Qarnayn, by
the right-guided Caliphs and impeccable leaders of Islam,
during their own times in different parts of the world.

---

6. Q, 28: 78.

VI. THE FALLACY OF MATERIALISM

Revolt against the Lord and Creator

It has been, indeed, one of the greatest misfortunes for the world as well as for humanity that the modern Western cultural impulses and ideas took shape at a time when the revolt against religion in general, and against the realities beyond the ken of human perception, had already captured the mind and heart of the Christian nations. The Western civilization was born and brought up amongst the nations which had entrenched themselves against a priestly order that exploited religion for the sake of base desires and selfish ends. In addition, an uncompromising opposition to worldly knowledge by the Christian Church had set its very face against the improvement of conditions of the earthly life. This coupled with the immorality, fanaticism, and ignorance of Church fathers, forced the people in the West to take a thoroughly anti-religious stand!

This, in its turn, gave a materialistic bias to endeavours of intellectual and cultural development, industrial progress, and social growth in these nations. As this lop-sided development increased, it also decreased the balance of a spiritual relationship between man and his Creator. All these consequences were, it would be seen, the product of inborn tendencies, temperaments, peculiar circumstances, and the social and religious order of the European peoples. This new civilization was thus born and raised in an atmosphere surcharged with atheistic and amoral tendencies. Phenomenal progress in the fields of physical sciences, industry and technology, on the other hand, enabled man to conquer space and set his foot on the moon.

An ever-increasing material progress, control over the forces of nature, and the dynamic expansion of human potentialities promising ultimate dominion over the universe, has, in consequence, given rise to an anti-God materialism which has become the champion of anti-religious thought and action. It is the distinctive mark and dominant characteristic of the modern materialistic civilization. We do not know of any other civilization so ruthlessly materialistic and at the same time so thoroughly God-opposing, hostile to everything divine in origin or religious in principle and method, craving for material power and pleasure, and claiming an unquestioning submission to its own impulses and ideas.

Culmination of the Materialistic Civilization

We have just stated that Western civilization has amassed immense material power and resources but is also God opposing traditionally, as well as in its make-up. Those who hold its reins are mainly motivated by the considerations of their own power and industrial progress, and are thus totally oblivious of everything except their own selfish ends. The intellectual centres of this civilization—America, Europe, and Russia—are overtly, and sometimes insidiously, at war with spirituality, unseen realities, religious ethics, and Divine over-lordship. The logical climax of this civilization, with its attendant materialism and industrial progress, does not appear to be far distant: its greatest champion and defender, *al-Dajjāl* in the prophetic language, shall soon make his debut.[1] He would necessarily be a God-opposing tyrant commanding all the resources of material and industrial progress, championing the cause of atheistic materialism, and

---

1. The Traditions predicting the appearance of al-Dajjāl clearly indicate his distinguishing features and characteristics. Being too numerous and handed down through different sources, these Traditions specify that al-Dajjāl would make his debut at a time fixed *aforehand* (although the time has not been made known to us) from amongst the Jews. The detailed references to the person and characteristics of al-Dajjāl hardly allow its denial or interpretation of the prophecies as alluding to *a seductive agency* and not to a definite person. These Traditions also specify that al-Dajjāl *will appear in Palestine* where he would wield immense power and glory. It seems that Palestine would be the last stage where this uncanny drama of struggle between faith and materialism will reach its final culmination. The makings of this sinister contest can even now be seen at work in the Holy Land. Facing the Jews, there is a nation whose greatest claim to power lies in its being custodian of the Divine Call to righteousness and the over-lordship of the One and Only God, while, on the other, there are the people believing in the superiority of race and blood. These adversaries of the faith in God and equality of mankind are bent upon employing the entire human and material resources of the world for establishing the undisputed superiority of their own race. And, they also hold the keys to the technological progress and the resources which lay at their door courtesy of the latest discoveries of physical sciences. The signs of this final encounter, crucial for humanity at large, and the Islamic East in particular, have already begun to manifest, only awaiting, perhaps, for the appointed time when the impending drama would unfold itself and a leading character as already mentioned in the prophesies, appears.

seeking divinity for the means of material prosperity and
for those who possess these means. This would be the
culminating point of this godless civilization which has
been brewed in the crucible of Europe for the past few
centuries.

Atheism, Dissension and Destruction

In the foregoing paragraph the essential features of the
present day materialistic-cum-industrial civilization, which
is soon likely to reach its climax, have been sketched.
Whenever that happens, its philosopher and guide shall be
no one else but al-Dajjāl. But, merely the leadership of a
materialistic civilization by someone does not offer
sufficient ground to identify him with al-Dajjāl: the anti-
God adversary of the Last Time who has been so bitterly
condemned by the Prophet of Islam, and from whose
appalling evils and calamities the believers have been asked
to seek the refuge of God! These directives by the Prophet
ṣallā Allāhu 'alayhi wasallam, to be sure, point out the
acuteness of the impending danger. Solomon once reigned
supreme and so did Dhū al-Qarnayn. The Qur'an speaks of
the immense material and political power owned by them
as well as the amazing speed and resources commanded by
them. We have, therefore, to discern clearly the dividing
line between them and al-Dajjāl, for this would form the
barrier between a tyrannical despot and a virtuous ruler
described thus by the Qur'an:

"How excellent a slave! Lo! he was ever turning

in repentance (toward Allah)." (Q, 38:30)

Now, this dominant characteristic of virtuous rulers, as indicated in the Qur'anic verse, constitutes the line of demarcation between such a suzerain and a tyrannical autocrat. Solomon and Dhū al-Qarnayn as well as most of the righteous and rightly-guided rulers presiding over the Islamic state during the first few centuries of its history, manifested this essential trait which always fostered an inspiration that directed their administrative skills, their political sagacity and brilliant capabilities, their sense of justice and love for humanity, towards the propagation of the true Faith. God has described their qualities as follows:

"Those, who, if We give them power in the land, establish worship and pay the poor-due and enjoin kindness and forbid iniquity. And Allah's is the sequel of events." (Q, 22:41)

"As for the Abode of the Hereafter We assign it unto those who seek not oppression in the earth, nor yet corruption. The sequel is for those who ward off (evil)." (Q, 28:83)

On the contrary, the most visible characteristic of al-Dajjāl, his identifying mark indicated by the Prophet of Islam, is atheism in its widest connotation. He said:

"KUFR (atheism) would be inscribed between his eyes. Every believer whether lettered or unlettered would be able to read that."[2]

---

2. *Ṣaḥīḥ al-Bukhārī.*

The Traditions of the Prophet clearly specify that al-Dajjāl would be an enthusiastic and crafty preacher of atheism and that his efforts would be directed to burden the believers with disbelief and scepticism. In another Tradition it has been stated that:

"By God, a man would come to him taking him to be a believer, and would become his follower. Then he would fall into scepticism prompted by the latter."[3]

The fascinating but hideous enchantment of al-Dajjāl would then spread out and envelop every family, hearth and home; neither women nor children would be immune from his hypnotizing spell; nobody would be able to exercise the needful restraint over his dependents, wife and children; everyone would be a law unto himself and would also be proud of it. A Tradition of the Prophet relates:

"Al-Dajjāl would sojourn in the barren lands of Marraqanat, where women would flock together to him, till the people would put their mothers, daughters, sisters and aunts into fetters lest they should also go over to him."[4]

The society would become so ethically barren and dissolute that:

"Only sinners and black sheep would at last remain who would be weightless like birds and empty-headed like beasts; and they would be unable to

3. *Abū Dā'ūd.*
4. *Al-Ṭabarānī*, on the authority of Ibn 'Umar.

distinguish between virtue and wickedness."[5]

This description of the modern materialistic and atheistic civilization depicts, in prophetic phraseology, the climax of this sophisticated and luxurious yet disintegrating culture. It also brings into relief the distinguishing features and the conspicuous traits of the present day society. This is, in truth and reality, one of those unfathomable miracles of the Prophet's teachings which shall ever continue to be a source of enlightenment and guidance to humanity. Who can deny the fact that the modern materialistic culture lacks depth and weight? It has not only unburdened itself of the weight of the gravest cares and responsibilities, but also learnt to fly in the sky like birds. Man has conquered both speed and space, but fails to live like human beings; he can destroy blooming gardens and plentiful crops, massacre entire nations with insufferable cruelty, and blot into extinction whole countries without the least hesitation. History is unable to cite any other civilization combining similar cruelty, barbarity, and inhumanity along with the abundance of goods and comforts. The Prophet of Islam alluded to the overflowing luxuries of the modern age in these words:

> "They would then have their provisions showering on them and shall have plentiful means of comfort.[6]

---

5. *Ṣaḥīḥ Muslim*, on the authority of ‘Abdullah ibn ‘Umar and Ibn al-‘Āṣ.
6. *Ṣaḥīḥ Muslim*, on the authority of ‘Abdullah ibn ‘Umar.

Fanciful Self-Satisfaction

We have explained how the concept of nature and society emanating from 'this-worldly' attitude, denies all other realities except the material world and the brief span of worldly life. It devotes its attention exclusively towards making this life more comfortable, prosperous, enchanting, and delightful, with complete disregard to social evils, moral morass, and the indescribable cruelty generated in its process. Divine revelation, therefore, comes up to show the cloven hoof of its standard-bearers in the concluding verses of Sūrat al-Kahf. The deeds and the personal bearings of these agents of death and destruction have been vividly delineated by the Qur'an, to spotlight their artful duplicity.

> "And when it is said unto them, Make not mischief
> in the earth, they say We are peace-makers only."
> (Q, 2:11)

This is a pointed allusion to the Jews who have completely forgotten the Resurrection and the Hereafter, despite the long-drawn-out chastisement they have undergone for past duplicity and treacherous behaviours. No doubt they have played a leading role in the development of physical sciences, industry and technology, but their contribution towards fomenting revolt and strife, instability and anarchy has also been without a parallel! On the whole, their endeavours, talents, and intellectual acumen have been directed more towards the negative ends, and have plunged the world into a moral and social confusion with the sole objective of asserting the superiority of their own "chosen race", over all other nations of the world.

> "Say: Shall We inform you who will be the greatest losers by their works? Those whose effort goes astray in the life of the world, and yet they reckon that they do good work. Those are they who disbelieve in the revelation of their Lord and in the meeting with Him. Therefore their works are vain, and on the Day of Resurrection We assign no weight to them." (Q, 18:103-5)

Limitation of Human Knowledge

The Qur'an protests against the materialistic view of epistemology which regards human intellect as infallible and capable of encompassing all phases of reality. This concept of knowledge asserts that it has the capacity to discern the secrets of nature as well as mysteries of the vast heavenly bodies and planetary system, of lands and oceans, of life and beings, and can penetrate the designs and workings of supernatural forces. It tries to plumb directly the secrets of the creation of life and unlock the mysteries of past and future. The votaries of this view of human knowledge are arrogantly proud of it, although the sum total of their knowledge is no more than a speck of dust. The tragedy, however, is that this very undue arrogance, over-confidence and excessive reliance on human knowledge, when coupled with the contemptuous defiance and outright denial of unseen realities, has been the root-cause of man's vanity and self-conceit, narrow-mindedness, and fanaticism. It is, indeed, this concept of human knowledge that is responsible for belief in the primacy of matter, its indestructibility, and self-generative properties.

It is, again, this view of human knowledge, having roots in an aberrant human nature that has always induced man to claim the dominion of his fellow beings, and to oppress those who do not agree to this concept. All of its salient features have been brought out by the parables told in Sūrat al-Kahf. For instance: its spiteful enmity with those who are blessed with a true faith and the gnosis of God, like the Companions of the Cave; its love of earthly possessions and disrespect for the poor and lowly as exhibited by the owner of two gardens; its denial of every thing not adequately comprehended by the limited human intellect, as illustrated by the story of al-Khiḍr and Moses. It is not infrequent that the erring knowledge of man produces an entirely false impression, such as Dhū al-Qarnayn thinking the sun had set in the spring of murky water.

"Till when he reached the setting-place of the sun,
he found it setting in a muddy spring." (Q, 18:86)

Another example of a similar delusion is furnished in the story of Solomon and the Queen of Sheba. The latter mistook the smooth polished floor of Solomon's palace and tucked up her trousers to pass through it.

"It was said unto her: Enter the hall. And when she

saw it she deemed it a pool and bared her legs. (Solomon) said: Lo! it is a hall, made smooth, of glass."[7] (Q, 27:44)

Sūrat al-Kahf ends with the same note with which it begins. It has been emphasised in the concluding verses that the Divine knowledge is immensely wider and deeper in comparison to that of man; that the Universe is much wider and greater than man can ever think of and the words[8] of the Lord—the words denoting His excellence, His attributes, and His perfection—can never be fully set out in human language, however developed it might be. Signs and commandments of God are infinite, and these cannot be expressed even if all the trees were made into pens and oceans[9] turned into ink.

---

7. The detail of the story of Solomon and the Queen of Sheba can be seen in the chapter *al-Namal* of the Qur'an.

8. Al-Alūsī has explained in *Rūḥ al-Ma'ānī* that the "words" mean the power, glory and wisdom of the Lord. Whenever God wants to express His mysteries and wonders, He simply gives the command Be—and the thing comes into being.

9. The astronomical observations of the expanding universe give us an idea of the immensity of space, the distance between the earth and the planets, as well as between different planets, their numbers, the speed of light, galaxies of heavenly bodies, their volumes and densities, the laws of gravity and the intricate interaction of physical laws sustaining the cosmos. Modern scientific discoveries also demonstrate how the rotation of earth, atmosphere of life-supporting gasses, the delicate proportion of life-giving elements and similar other phenomenal cause go to make this earth habitable and life-sustaining. Numerous other branches of science like biology, chemistry, zoology, botany and other physical sciences have revealed, thanks to well-equipped laboratories and the toils of innumerable intelligent scientists, what could have never been conceived a few centuries ago. But all this

"Say: Though the sea became ink for the Words of
My Lord, verily the sea would be used up before
the Words of my Lord were exhausted, even
though We brought the like thereof to help." (Q,
18:109)

Again, Sūrat Luqmān says:

"And if all the trees in the earth were pens, and the
sea, with seven more seas to help it, (were ink), the
Words of Allah could not be exhausted. Lo! Allah
is Mighty, Wise." (Q, 31:27)

Prophethood: Its Nature and Necessity

A question arises here. If the universe and the innumerable
creations contained therein are beyond human imagination;
if all the trees and seven seas are inadequate to expound the
wisdom and glory of God; and if the infinite signs and
commandments of the Lord are beyond the ken of human
understanding; then how can man attain the knowledge of
His excellence and His attributes? How can the mystery of
life be solved, and how is man to seek the path of Divine
guidance and righteousness? The prophets too are no more
than mere mortals. We know that the knowledge of man is
extremely limited and liable to err. Then how are we to
place reliance on the teachings and wisdom of a prophet?
The Sūrah reveals the answer to all these questions on

---

knowledge is infinitesimally small as compared to the knowledge still beyond
our reach.

behalf of the last Prophet of God:

> "Say: I am only a mortal like you. My Lord inspires in me that your God is only One God." (Q, 18:110)

This verse tells us that the only reliable source of God's gnosis—the means to fathom the mystery of mysteries and also the mark of honour and excellence of the prophets—is the revelation vouchsafed to them. Man can never aspire to attain enduring success without placing reliance in the prophetic inspiration. This was the quintessence and central truth of prophethood expounded by the Prophet of Islam, when he said: "I am only a mortal like you. My Lord inspires in me that your God is only one God."

The Last Word

The Sūrah concludes by drawing our attention again towards the Hereafter and its paramount importance for our worldly life. It calls upon us to always keep this fundamental truth in view and draw inspiration from it in all our actions and demeanour. The Sūrah thus concludes with the message it expounded in the opening verses:

> "And whoever hopes for the meeting with his Lord, let him do righteous work, and make none sharer of the worship due unto his Lord." (Q, 18:110)

BIBLIOGRAPHY

1   Abul Kalām Āzād, *Tarjumān al-Qur'ān*, Medina Press, Bijnor.

2.   Sayyidd Abul A'la Mawdudi, *Tafhīm al-Qur'ān*, vol. III, Delhi (1965).

3.   Shahāb al-Dīn al-Sayyid Muhammad al-Alūsī, *Rūḥ al-Ma'ānī*, (Tafsīr al-Qur'ān al-'Aẓīm), Cairo, (1353 A. H.).

4.   'Imād al-Dīn Abul Fidā' Ismā'īl ibn 'Umar ibn Kathīr, *Tafsīr Ibn Kathīr*, Cairo (1356 /1937).

5.   Imām Fakhr al-Dīn al-Rāzī, *al-Tafsīr al-Kabīr*, vol, III, Cairo (1324 A. H.).

6.   Imām Abū Ja'far Muhammad ibn Jarīr al-Ṭabarī, *Tafsīr Ibn Jarīr* (*Jāmi' al-Bayān fī Tafsīr al-Qur'ān*), Al-Maṭba'ah Maimanah, Cairo (1321 A. H.).

7.   Muhammad Jamāluddīn al-Qāsimī, *al-Tafsīr al-Qāsmī* (*Maḥāsin al-Tā'wīl*) Cairo (1380 /1960).

8.   Sayyid Quṭub, *Fī Ẓilāl al-Qur'ān*, Kuwait (1386/1967).

9.   Abū 'Abdullah Muhammad ibn Ismā'īl al-Bukhārī, *Ṣaḥīḥ al-Bukhārī*, Delhi, (1354 A. H.).

10.   Abu 'Abdullah Muhammad ibn 'Abdullah Al-Hākim Nishapuri, *al-Mustadrak lil-Ḥākim*, Dā'iratul-Ma'ārif, Hyderabad, (1334 A. H.).

11.   Abul Husain Muslim ibn al-Hajjāj al-Qushayrī, *Ṣaḥīḥ Muslim*, Delhi.

12.   Abu 'Isā Muhammad ibn 'Isā al-Tirmidhī, *Jāmi' al-Tirmidhī*.

13.   Imām Ahmad Ibn Hanbal, *Musnad Aḥmad*.

14.   Abul Hasan al-Darqaṭnī, *Kitāb al-Sunan*.

15. Al-Ḥāfiẓ Sulaymān ibn Sulaymān al-Ṭabarānī, *Mu'jam al-Ṭabrānī.*

16. Ibn al-Jawzī, *Ṣifat al-Ṣafwah*, vol. I, Hyderabad, (1335 A. H.).

17. Abul Faḍal, Jamāluddin Muhammad ibn Mukarram ibn Manẓūr, *Lisān al-'Arab,* al-Maṭba'ah al-Kubrā al-Mīriyah, Bulaq, Cairo (1300 A. H.).

18. Imām Abū 'Abdulrahmān Ahmad ibn Shu'ayb al-Nasā'ī, *Nasā'ī.*

19. Imām Muhammad ibn Yazīd ibn Mājah al-Qazwīnī, *Sunan Ibn Mājah.*

20. Sayyid Manāzir Ahsan, Gīlānī, *Tafsīr Sūrat al-Kahf,* Lucknow.

21. Shāh Walliullah Dehlavi, *Ḥujjatullah al-Bālighah*, Egypt, (1351 A. H.).

22. Sulaymān ibn al-Ash'ath al-Sijistānī, *Sunan Abī Dā'ūd.*

23. Abū Hāmid ibn Muhammad al-Ghazālī, *Iḥyā' 'Ulūm al-Dīn*, Egypt, (1346 A. H.).

24. Shaykh al-Islām Taqī al-Din ibn Taymiyyah, *Al-Jawāb al-Ṣaḥīḥ liman baddala Dīn al-Masīḥ,* Maṭba'at al-Nīl, Egypt, (1323/1905).

25. Shaykh al-Islām Taqī al-Dīn ibn Taymiyyah, *Tafsīr Sūrat al-Ikhlāṣ*, al-Matba'ah al-Husayniyyah, Egypt, (1323 A. H.).

26. Shaykh Muhammad Ṭāhir Patnī Gujarātī, *Majma' Biḥār al-Anwār*, Newal Kishore Press, Lucknow, (1283 A. H.).

27. Edward Gibbon, *Decline and Fall of the Roman Empire*, vols. I, II and III, London, (1908).

28. Blackie, *A Manual of Bible History.*

29. George H. Dyer, *A History of Christian Church*, vol. I, New York, (1896).

30. *Historians History of the World*, vol. VI, London, (1908).

31. J. A. Hammerton, *Universal History of the World*, vol. II.

32. *Encyclopaedia Britannica*, vol. I, (1968).
33. *Encyclopaedia of Religion and Ethics*, vol. XI, (1938).
34, Marmaduke Pickthall, *The Meaning of Glorious Qur'an*, Bangalore, (1952).
35. S. Abul Hasan Ali Nadwī, *Islam and the World*, Lucknow, (1967)

INDEX